16 Boultwood Road, Beckton, E65QQ

Disclaimer:

Every effort has been made to check the contents of this book for accuracy. However, the authors recommend that you always consult an independent financial adviser before buying a house. The information used and decisions taken are entirely at your own risk. House prices can go up as well as go down, and your house may be repossessed if you do not keep up with your mortgage repayments. The contents of this book are based on the authors' research and do not constitute financial advice. The authors cannot be held responsible for the results of action, inaction, or otherwise taken as a consequence of the information in this book. All the Internet addresses (URLs) contained within this book are valid at the time of going to press. However, due to the dynamic nature of the Internet, some addresses may change, and some sites may alter or cease to exist, post-publication. Whilst the authors and publishers regret any inconvenience this may cause readers, either the authors or publishers can accept no responsibility for any such changes.

GW00730611

About the Author

To many potential house buyers, the purchase of a property in the UK is considered an extremely difficult and risky process, a view related in many cases to the experiences of buying property in other countries. Many buyers are not aware of the protection available, the savings to be made and the benefits to be obtained from buying property in the UK. Purchasing property in the UK can be both a wise and profitable investment. This guide will lead you through the rules, regulations and secrets of getting on the property ladder. Along the way, we will show you what to do and what not to do to make sure that your property purchase turns into a sound investment.

Daily Express Saturday August 9 2008 23

LONDON: Fadi Safieddine paid £185,000 for a £230,000 house

Pictures: STEVE FRANK, JOHN NGUYEN, JOHN ROBERTSON

negotiate
nerous
scounts

Fadi Safieddine, 34, lecturer in computer studies, bought a two-bedroom home in Beckton

"I had been waiting a long time for a two-bedroom house to come on the market in this area at less than £250,000. I watched the market and kept contacting agents and then, finally, it happened.

My vendor had been wanting to sell before the crash and put her place on the market then for £230,000 but we negotiated her down to £185,000, which was seriously below the market price for that area. I've lived in London for 11 years and have been saving my deposit. I had a mortgage pre-arranged with the Woolwich and a back-up

'I am aware that the market could fall further but I don't intend to sell and my job is safe'

Pictures by
Aleksey Lapkovsky

arranged with HSBC, so I was well placed to buy quickly.

This area is getting a lot of investment because of the Olympics. It's a nice, quiet street and Beckon Park is just a minute's walk away. The house needed decorating but I could see the potential. I just needed to replace the

floors with wood and put in double-glazed doors and windows. I have got them all for £2,400. This market means that goods are cheaper and often the work to fit them is thrown in. I bought them on Monday and they were all fitted on Thursday.

I am aware that the market could fall further, and if prices crash more than 30 per cent I will be in negative equity but I don't intend to sell and my job is safe. My rent before was £780 a month for one bedroom in Dagenham; my mortgage is £760 for two bedrooms closer to London and to work, so I'm just over the moon."

Fadi Safieddine negotiated the price of his two-bedroom house with garden in Beckton down from £230,00 to £185,000

Dr. Fadi Safieddine is an associate professor in MIS and Computer Science. He completed his PhD in 2004 at the University of East London in E-commerce. He has been directly involved in buying and selling properties in the UK for some years and turned an initial £8,000 investment in his first house into £132,000 in just seven years. This biggest payoff came during the boom in the housing market. A second property, purchased with a deposit of £30,000 had increased in value to a £220,000 eight years later, a period of time that coincided with the UK property crash of 2008. During that crash, Dr Safieddine was able to negotiate a remarkable deal on his purchase, an achievement reported by no less than three local and national newspapers.

hard before ever having a mortgage again. It's been a nightmare.

THE BARGAIN HUNTER

FADI SAFIEDDINE, 34, a lecturer in computer studies, recently bought a two-bedroom home in Beckton, East London.

FADI says: I was looking to buy a house nearer my work and had calculated what I could afford. I had been waiting a long time for a two-bedroom house to come on the market in this area at less than £250,000 so I could also avoid the next band of stamp duty.

This property was on the market for £230,000. The vendor was moving jobs and had to sell but when my offer of only £185,000 was accepted I couldn't believe it. Even allowing for the fall in prices that's seriously below the market value for the area.

I'm paying £760 a month for the mortgage but I'd have to pay £900 to rent a similar property. I definitely believe I got a bargain. Prices would have to crash a long way for me to be in negative equity and I intend to live here for several years. Because I'm closer to work I'm selling my car, which will save me more money.

My new house is in a quiet street near a big park. It needed decorating but I could see the potential. Because I'm in a secure job and was putting down a good sized deposit I was also able to get a good mortgage deal. All round, I think I've done well and showed it is possible to make the market work in your favour.

Reading this book will increase your knowledge in the world of house buying. The authors' hope, however, those readers who follow the steps and the advice given to increase their chances of turning their property purchase into a profitable investment.

Whilst this guide is primarily aimed at the homeowner, that is buyers who wish to live in their property, the information contained here is also relevant to property investors. It should be pointed that people are investing rather than buying to live in the property take potentially greater risks than homebuyers.

Acknowledgement:

We would like to thank Mr Mike Kretsis (Senior Lecturer) for his valuable in- put. We would like to also thank Edmund Archibald for the author's photos.

Table of Contents

Chapter 1: Why is buying almost always better than renting?

In this chapter, we will outline why buying is almost always a safe investment. We will also outline some key facts unknown by many people living in the UK and why people are wasting so much money paying rent when they could be paying less and keeping that money safe in their property as an investment.

W hy do many people think that buying a house is risky?

Why do they keep paying rent and inflating landlords' income instead of keeping much of their hard earned money for themselves? Of even more concern is the question, 'Why pay so much rent when you can pay less in monthly mortgage payments?' How is it that some people who invest little end-up making so much more money even when house prices do not change or go down? There are probably a large number of answers to these questions, but we believe that the single, most

> **Fact 1:**
>
> You do not need to be a British National to get a loan to buy a house in the UK.

important factor is a lack of information available to people. You can buy a house with a bank loan, almost risk free, even if you are not a British national. Whilst there are some guides available, the language used in them is very technical. This guide sets out to show you how to buy, what the real risks are, how to avoid those risks, and how to complete the process of purchasing confident of a successful outcome.

YOU ALREADY PAY TO LIVE IN YOUR PROPERTY, RIGHT? The first and most obvious benefit of owning your own property is saving money. Anyone who does not own a property will tell you that rents are too high and are continually increasing. If you have a stable income, even as self-employed, and you can afford to pay the rent then you will be able to invest in your own home using a bank loan, better known as a 'mortgage'.

1.1: What is a Mortgage?

In simple terms, a mortgage is a loan that you get from the bank to buy a house. The bank part-owns the house with you. You cannot, therefore, sell the house without paying the outstanding amount of the loan to the bank. Banks expect certain criteria to be met before giving you a mortgage. Being a UK national helps but is not essential because the risk to the bank is limited.

Unlike cars and other movable objects, you cannot 'pack' the house and runaway with the house abroad. So the risk to the bank is very limited. There are several types of mortgages, but only two or three are really worthwhile. Later on, we will be discussing in detail the best mortgages and which ones will suit you. For now, we will consider the UK's most popular choice amongst homeowners, the repayment mortgage.

Repayment Mortgages:

Repayment mortgages are no different from any other loan. You borrow money and pay back both interest and part of the loan every month.

Take a real example of a two-bedroom house in east London. In Zone 3, a typical mortgage payment is currently £850 a month. Of this £850, on average, £400 in interest, and the remaining £450 is put towards the actual owning the house. So every month you pay, you own another £450 of the house. You could think of it as owning 'few more bricks' of the house. But the point is that you OWN it. If you ever sell the house, you get that money back.

Fact 2:

UK banks carry a minimal risk when giving you a mortgage.

There are many other types of mortgages and mortgage options which we will discuss in Chapter Two, Section 2.6. In the meantime, let us highlight some other relevant facts about house buying.

1.2: Why banks are happy to lend you money

As we mentioned before a mortgage is just a type of loan given by the banks. However, from the banks' point of view, it is one of the most secure forms of loans they can give. Without their permission, a house cannot be sold because they are part owners of the property. Some banks will also require homeowners to take out buildings insurance so that, in the event of a disaster or accident such as a fire, subsidence or flood, the property is insured and the insurance company will compensate you and the bank. Given the above, the only situation in which, realistically, a bank is likely to lose money on a mortgage loan would occur if the homeowner defaulted (stops paying back) on his or her mortgage payments. In such a situation, and as a last resort, a bank will seek to repossess the house. As you would expect in a mature market like the UK, banks and the government, have made sure there is a clearly defined and established process governing the repossession of houses. Banks have no interest in repossessing a house unless they have absolutely no other choice. For this to happen, banks are required by law to issue at least three warnings, which could take from three to six months. After this, they must seek repossession through courts. Sending the necessary documents to the courts typically takes another three to six months. The entire process could take as much as a year at which point, the court will normally grant the bank repossession of the house. Meanwhile, the house owner has at his or her disposal some options (explained in the next sections), which will avoid the repossession of the house. At any point during the year, if the borrower restarts mortgage payments the repossession process automatically stops. However, the borrower's credit history will be badly affected, an issue which we will discuss in chapter three. It makes sense therefore that, as a homeowner, you maintain your mortgage payments at all costs.

Credit History:

> Credit History is your financial history since you first open a bank account in the UK. Credit History keeps track of your payment history, bank history, credit card history, and any penalty for late payments or defaulted payments.

Here is how the UK banks reduce the risks associated with mortgage loans. You will find when you apply for a mortgage that banks will ask for a down payment also called a 'deposit'. This deposit is usually between 5% and 10% of the house price and which is paid by the homeowner at the start of the mortgage. At the time of the house purchase, the buyer effectively owns a proportion of the house equivalent to the value of the deposit paid. This deposit is a 'buffer' that protects the bank. If for any reason the house owner stops payment of his/her mortgage, the bank is unlikely to start losing money on the property even if it takes time to repossess the house and then sell it. You, however, will likely to lose your 5% to 10% deposit. If the bank sells the house for exactly the same price for which you bought it, the bank will return your deposit minus their expenses for selling the house. If the bank sells it for more than the original price, you will receive your deposit plus the difference between the original and selling price (of course minus the bank's expenses). If the bank sells it at less than the original price, then it will deduct the loss from your deposit and return the difference to you. In rare cases, banks may even charge you for the difference although they are most likely to simply write it off as a loss.

We will show you in this book how to avoid these scenarios. In fact, we will show you how to ensure that you always profit from your house purchases and never end up losing your house, regardless of your personal circumstances or the state of the UK property market. Indeed, it is worth remembering that wise investors were able to make significant profits even during the house price crash, which occurred a few years ago.

Fact 3:

Mortgages are the safest loan a bank can give. A house owner cannot take his house with them, unlike the case with car loans, credit cards, and other loans.

It is important to appreciate that getting a mortgage is relatively easy. Banks make significant profits from mortgage loans, so it is in their interests to lend you money. To illustrate this incentive, take the following example: A 30 years' of monthly mortgage repayments on a £155,000 property at a 5.2% interest rate would yield a profit for the bank of £151 000[1]. That is almost the price of the house! However, from the homeowner's perspective, this mortgage is still much cheaper than renting the same property over the same period. That same property would cost £1,100 per month to rent. Now if we multiply that by 12 (months per year) times 30 (years), which equals £396,000. This is a huge sum of money to pay for something that you will never own.

---

[1] Remember this is a repayment mortgage so the capital goes down every month. If the house owner selects an interest-only mortgage then the payments are less every month but ultimately over 30 years, the house owner pays much more i.e. 5.2% x 30 years x 155,000 = £251,000.

1.3: How homeowners make money?

To learn how homeowners make money from their property;
you need to learn about something called "Equity".

> *Equity is the proportion of your house that you own.*
> *The first piece of equity that you own corresponds to*
> *the money that you put down as a 'deposit'.*

But a deposit is just one part of the equity. Every month you
pay your mortgage, you own that little bit more of your
house. That few more 'bricks' of the house are now yours. So
the second way homeowners build equity in their property is
by paying their mortgage and the repayment of the house in
that process. The third way in which homeowners make
money occurs when the value of their property increases.
Whilst there are no guarantees that property prices will rise in
the short term, historically the trend over a period of several
years is almost always in an upward direction. We will now
examine the issue of equity in more detail.

So let's see, step by step, how a house owner makes a profit
and how slowly homeowner starts owning the property. See
figure 1.1 for guidance.

Firstly, when the house owner buys the property, the
homeowner has to pay a deposit.

The deposit represents the first small part of the house that they own. With every monthly payment, the homeowners own a few more 'pieces' of the house. These pieces do not amount to a great deal initially because homeowners pay more in interest than in repayments. But as the months and years pass by, the homeowners will start to own more and more of the house.

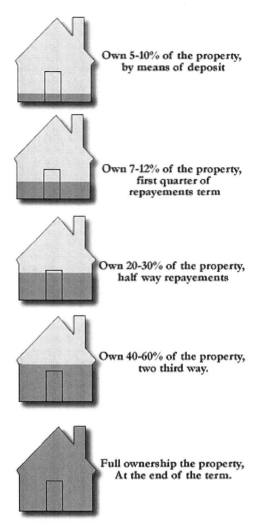

Own 5-10% of the property, by means of deposit

Own 7-12% of the property, first quarter of repayements term

Own 20-30% of the property, half way repayements

Own 40-60% of the property, two third way.

Full ownership the property, At the end of the term.

How quickly the homeowner will own the house in its entirety will depend upon the number of years over which they agreed with the bank to pay off the mortgage. This period of time is referred to as the repayment period.

Figure 1.1. Owning your home

The repayment period is the length of time, agreed with the bank, over which you pay back the mortgage loan. This period is usually between 15 years and 40 years.

Of course, if the house owner can afford to pay off the mortgage sooner than the end of the repayment period, then they should try to do so. The faster you pay the mortgage, the quicker you will own the house and the less interest you will incur. However, as the table below shows, to borrow £150,000 at 5% interest, the change in repayment years can make a significant difference to the house owner's monthly repayments.

Repayment Years	Monthly Mortgage
15 years	£1,186 a month
20 Years	£989.93
30 Years	£805.23
40 Years	£723.29

Take the real example of the house in east London, identified in Section 1.1. Purchased in 2008 at £185,000, the homeowner put down £40,000 as a deposit. He could have put down less as the bank required only 10% (or £18,500) but he could afford to pay more. Automatically, from day one, this house owner owns 21.5% of the house, i.e. 40,000÷185,000 × 100. If at any time in the future he sells the house for the same price or higher, he will get back his £40,000 deposit and potentially more. The monthly repayments at an interest rate of 5.2% for 30 years equal £850.

Fact 4:

The longer the mortgage, the lower the monthly payments but, the longer it will take for the house owner to own the house in its entirety.

Let us assume that this homeowner lives in the house for six years. Keeping in mind that the rent for similar properties in that area is £1100 per month, monthly mortgage repayments of £850 represent a significant saving. Of the £850 per month, the owner is paying the bank £400 in interest, and the remaining £450 is going as a 'repayment' to the house. With every month, he owns another £450 of the house. In a year, he owns £5,400 of the house whilst in six years, he has not only saved £18,000 (£250 per month – the difference between his monthly mortgage repayments and the rent for a similar property - times 12 months times 6 years), but this homeowner has also paid off a total of £32,400 of the value of the house. On the 6th anniversary of moving in, this house owner owns now £32,400 or 21% of his house and has saved £18,000 in rent. **This is the shocking moment when you realise that two people, one renting and one owning for six years will see the homeowner better off by £50,400!**

As if this was not a reason enough to celebrate, house prices have, in the meantime, would more likely go up. In 2016 the value of the house example we mentioned has gone up to £295,000. Bearing in mind that the eight years between 2008 and 2016 were difficult years for the UK housing market; this house owner was able to make £115,000 on his initial investment by effectively doing nothing other than relaxing and living in that house. In total, by buying as opposed to renting over the eight-year period, this homeowner has increased the value of his investment by £147,400 and has also saved £18,000 in rents. This example is replicated in many places across the UK. However, in later chapters, we will show you two very unusual cases in which house prices went down rather than up. We will also explain what you should do in such rare circumstances.

1.4: Applying for a mortgage

Anyone can apply for mortgage providing they meet certain conditions. The most important condition is income. House owners have to prove that they have money coming in. Mortgage companies are looking for the source of your income, especially payslips. Your salary shown on payslips are highly regarded. The amount of money coming in every month will show them whether or not you will able to keep up with your mortgage payments. Mortgage companies also look for outgoings, for example, how much is paid to credit card companies, to loans, or other commitments. If your outgoings are significant, then your application might be declined. But it is important to remember that you already can afford the rent so surely you should be able to pay a mortgage, especially if it is less than the rent.

However, income might be declared in other ways and not only by salary. If the homeowner is self-employed, an independent trader, contract working, working part-time, or has a partner who works then all these are counted as other

> *Fact 5:*
>
> Any money coming in as income on a regular basis can be put forward as a source of income when applying for a mortgage.

sources of income. If steady income can be shown in bank statements for at least a year and taxes have been paid, then the bank will usually be happy to offer the homeowner a mortgage.

If you are an independent trade person without a fixed income but one that goes up massively at times and goes down at other times, you are considered to be risky. There are ways to reduce these risks. Options you may want to consider include making 'over' payments, 'under' payments and even taking payment holidays. 'Over' payment means that the house owner pays three or four months in advance or even a year in advance because he has large amounts of spare cash. Should the house owner subsequently come across a period when business is slow, he can take few months payment holiday as they have already paid the next few months in advance. This is a well-established way of paying and an option many banks offer their customers. There is also an option of taking out mortgage payment insurance and looking at what the British government offers all UK residents. All of these options will be explained later in this book.

A permanent job and salary income of three-six months are enough to get an offer of a mortgage. The banks can tell you in advance how much they are willing to lend you, and they will give you a written confirmation to that effect. Having a paper from the bank confirming how much they are willing to lend you puts you in a stronger position when hunting for a house.

1.5: The Amount to borrow

At the time of writing this book, the maximum amount of lending usually would be four times the annual income of the homeowner. However, some of the banks will offer up to five times while others will only offer three times. It is worth shopping around if you need a big loan. For example, if the homeowner's salary is £25 000 then most UK banks will allow them to borrow between £100 000 to £125 000. This does not mean that this is the price of the house they are limited to. With the deposit on top of their mortgage, they can look for properties between £110,000 and £137,000. If this is not enough to buy a flat or a house, then they need to consider their partner's income, as two incomes are always better than one. A couple with a combined income of say £40,000 can borrow £160,000 to £200,000. Now you can see the difference. Some homeowners buy a two bedroom house or flat and rent one of the bedrooms to help top up their income, an option some couples who separate end up doing. Before new homeowners decide to buy a house, it is important that they DO NOT apply for a mortgage unless they are absolutely sure they will be accepted. If the homeowner gets rejected this will reduce their chances of getting a mortgage later on, and banks may subsequently charge them higher interest rates. Later in this book, we will outline exactly what steps you should take to check your credit history and how to make sure that the first bank you apply to will definitely give you a 'yes' answer. If you do not follow these steps correctly, you risk getting your application rejected. Once it is rejected, it will be much harder to get another mortgage offer at a good rate.

1.6: Things that can affect your application

There are many things that can affect your mortgage application. Good income, having a good deposit and good credit history are extremely important. Of course not having a good income, any deposit, and poor credit history are not going to help but later in this book we will show you how you can overcome many of these problems legally.

Fact 6:

Homeowners should never apply for a mortgage unless they are sure they can get an acceptance. Rejection by a bank will make future applications more difficult

But there are things that affect your application negatively. If the homeowner has too many loans, too many debts, many children to look after, and unemployed family members who will be staying in the property, all this will reduce the amount of money the banks would be willing to lend.

If the homeowner has been refused a loan or gets declined for a mortgage for any reason, this usually makes it harder to get a mortgage later on. So it is essential that before the homeowner applies for their very first mortgage they are sure that they will be accepted, even for as little as a £50,000 mortgage loan. Otherwise, they should not apply at all and wait for their credit history and other factors to improve.

The subsequent chapter dedicated to how all your criteria are checked and to identify exactly what credit history that banks are able to see, including your chances of being accepted before you apply, is absolute essential reading before you make your first application.

According to the Guardian newspaper (Chalabi, 2013), between 2008/2010 9.2 million-house owners in the UK had mortgages yet according to the Council of Mortgage Lenders in the UK, repossession was less than 0.06% in 2013 (CML, 2013). This means that less than 57,000 houses are repossessed that year. This might look like a large number but out of 9.2 million mortgage house owners, this is not a lot.

1.7: Fear of owning a property

There are always concerns when it comes to buying your first house. Many people, who have no experience of how this process works, get consumed by highly exaggerated stories and forget that for the absolute majority owning a property is the best investment they have ever made. We hope to address all these concerns one by one.

Here are some the main the questions that worried homeowners have:

- Will I lose my house?
- Will I go to jail if I do not pay my mortgage?
- What if the house has structural problems, fire or needs major repair?
- If I lose my job, what do I do?
- If I want to leave the country in the short term, long-term, or permanently, what do I do?
- What if my income goes up or goes down, what do I do then?
- What if house prices crash?
- What if the interest rates go up?

You've probably noticed that we have covered some of these questions already but let us have a final review of them.

1.7.1: Will I lose my house?

There is always a risk of losing your house, but there are many factors which make this less likely. The banks genuinely do not want to take away a house from its owner. It will mean that they will lose the interest they have been generating from the mortgage. They will have to go through a long court process to get their hands on the house, and they will have pay legal, repossession and selling costs via estate agents.

Banks will not go down the route of repossessing the house unless they have to. There is only one case in which they would do that if the house owner stops paying their mortgage and does not make the immediate arrangements that we will outline at the end of this chapter.

1.7.2: Will I go to jail if I do not pay my mortgage?

We would say almost never. The legal system in the UK considers all cases of financial difficulty as civil matters. They are not 'criminal' matters and as such do not have jail sentences associated with them. Courts in the UK, when finding that house owners have not paid their mortgage; will issue county court judgments against them.

This usually affects the homeowner's credit history for a very long time. If a house is repossessed and the price of it drops significantly, the most a civil court would give the homeowner is a negative credit mark on their record, which will affect her credit history badly. This will make it almost impossible to apply for future credit cards, loans and mortgages. If the homeowner has existing mortgages, the next time they have to renew them the interest rate would likely be very high. That is why it is very important to make sure that mortgage repayments are paid and are paid on time. We did say almost never. In extremely rare cases, individuals could end up in jail. For example, when a person lies in their application, is involved in criminal activities or where part of the property purchase is used for the purposes of money laundering. These cases are so rare that there are no official statistics of the number of people going to jail because of them.

Fact 7:

Get building insurance, life insurance and critical illness insurance, does not cost much and could save you a lot of money if things go wrong.

1.7.3: What if the house has structural problems burns down or needs major repair?

A tenant knows that if something goes wrong, they can ring the landlord to fix it. If the house has major problems, it is the landlord's problem and responsibility. While this is a nice feeling to have, it is far too expensive compared to owning your own property. There are ways homeowners can do to protect themselves from these problems.

Firstly, properties in the UK are built to very high standards. Properties go through rigorous health and safety checks before being approved. Structurally you can be assured that most homes are of a very good standard. Also, before banks approve a mortgage, they will insist on a home search and a structural inspection of the property, paid by the homeowner and usually between £200 to £500 depending on the size of the property.

The final and extremely important thing you need to do before you buy the house is to get building insurance. Be careful not to confuse this with home insurance, which is protecting the content of the property. Building insurance protects your building in case of fire, subsidence (the building tilting), major structural problems or if an aeroplane falls out of the sky on your house! The building insurance for a property of £200,000 can be as little as £13.00 a month. Some combine this with life and critical illness insurance. This means the homeowner can ensure that should they die or become critically ill; the insurance company will pay off the whole mortgage so that the person's family can continue to live in the house without any worries. Life and critical illness insurance for a property of £200,000 can be as little as £50 a month. This is a very small cost to making sure you live in your home worry and stress-free.

1.7.4: If I lose my job, what do I do?

The first thing to do is to register as unemployed at a job seekers' centre immediately. The centre will get the ball rolling and will arrange some financial support whilst you get another job. This includes paying the interest on your mortgage if you are unable to find a job after 12 weeks. The centre will also give you documentation and instructions which you can give to your bank. These documents will ask the bank to stop repayments on your mortgage and charge you just interest. The government does not want you to lose your home because if you become homeless then you become their problem and that will cost the government a lot more. So going back to the example of the house in east London with a monthly mortgage of £850, which included £400 interest and £450 repayment, every month, the government will pay the £400, and the bank will stop asking for £450 while you find another job. The job centre will not pay your other loans or if you have borrowed more money on your mortgage. They will only pay the 'interest' on the original mortgage you got on the house.

> *Fact 8:*
> Losing your job does not mean losing your house.

As standard, banks will not even question your request, and they will be happy to accept this agreement however long it takes. As indicated before, banks have no interest in repossessing your property. So really there are no major risks of losing your house if you act quickly. You should immediately get in touch with the jobcentre even if you have enough money for a few months. The process may take time, and this financial support is available to all UK residents.

1.7.5: If I want to leave the country in the short term, long-term or permanently, what do I do?

Put the house up for rent. As many tenants know, the demand for rented housing is very high. There are very few places in the UK that struggle to find tenants. What is more, the absolute majority of properties are rented at a price that is higher than the corresponding mortgage. Therefore the homeowner can leave at any time they want and still make money. To manage the property, they can contact and arrange with property management agent. There are many of them in every town and city. Homeowners will be making some money every month, but the real money is the repayment of the house and the fact the house is likely to go up in value. If the house owner does not intend to come back at all, then they might consider selling it.

1.7.6: What if my income goes up or goes down, what do I do?

You can always negotiate with your bank to increase or reduce the number of years of repayment. Go back to Table 1.1 and consider if you can make larger payments thereby reducing the number of years until you own the property. If your situation gets worse, you can ask the bank to increase the repayment years. If you know from the start that there will be some variability in your income, then you need, from the start, to make sure that your mortgage is flexible and allows both over and underpayments and even payment holidays. There are many banks that welcome such arrangements.

1.7.7: What if house prices crash?

Since 1973, property prices in the UK have gone up much more than they have gone down. And while there have been a few drops, the overall trend has always been upwards as the diagram below shows.

(Daily Mail, 2013)

There is some consolation in knowing that the UK economy is a mature economy when it comes to house ownership. The UK government is very experienced in protecting homeowners. When the last house price crash happened in 2008, an event often referred to as the credit crunch, the UK government and the Bank of England took serious measures to protect homeowners. Some of these measures you already have read about them here, such as protecting people who lose their jobs. But also they went as far as dropping interest rates to a historically low 0.25% to keep the majority of mortgages affordable. No actions at any point were taken that would have put at risk of losing people's homes that the 9.5 million mortgage holders and their dependents live in. These mortgage holders and dependents represent some 38% of the total UK population. This 38 % represent significant portion of voters that UK government are very careful to not upset.

Fact 9:

A property is a valuable asset in the UK. There are many ways you can make money from it.

The key point that a homeowner should bear in mind is that paying off the mortgage is very important but that the mortgage is still cheaper than paying rent. With that in mind, the only time the homeowner needs to be concerned is when they decide to sell. For half a million mortgage-homeowners who were left with negative equity in 2008, the difference between before and after the crash is psychological only. Those who freaked out and sold their property ended up losing money. Those who just stayed put and enjoyed their home and paid the mortgage are likely to be, in 2017, enjoying a house that is significantly back in profit. On top of this, these homeowners have saved money by paying their mortgage rather than renting for so many years.

The reason why house prices in the United Kingdom are less likely to go down massively is because it is very hard to get permission to build new houses and flats. The land is very expensive. New developments have to meet very strict requirements set by the British government and EU regulations – including matching the design of other nearby properties, getting permission from all the neighbours, making sure there is enough building space and ensuring that adequate parks, transport, schools and other facilities exist for the people moving in the area. New homeowners should not be concerned about drops in prices that they may have witnessed in other parts of Europe. Ultimately, homeowners will save significantly by paying less in mortgage repayments than in rent provided, of course, they should make sure before they buy that the cost of mortgage repayment is lower than the corresponding rent. This issue will be discussed thoroughly later in this book.

1.7.8: What if the interest rates go up?

Interest rates can go up and down. Naturally, homeowners do get worried if the interest rate goes up because it may mean that their mortgages might go up. We emphasise here 'may mean' and 'might' because there are choices here that a house owner can make. They can for instance switch to an interest-only rate, which is not ideal because the homeowner is not paying off the mortgage anymore but just the interest. This means it will take longer for the homeowner to own the house but this is always better than putting the homeowner under financial pressure. There are other options, some of which we have already mentioned, such as renting the house out. Here are other possible options:

1- **Rent one of the rooms out:** It is not unusual to rent a room out. There are many agencies and even websites that can help you rent a room. For example, Gumtree.com, Craigslist and even some agencies would be interested. If you live near a college or university, you may be able to rent to a student. The 'rent a room scheme' by the UK Tax Office means you can rent the room and pay no tax on the first £7,500 a year. You will find that there are few places in the UK where you would exceed that level of rent from a room. (GOV.UK, 2017). Some websites will let you list your room, e.g. spareroom.co.uk, roombuddies.co.uk, homestay.com, uk.easyroommate.com and housepals.co.uk. You will find many more sites online. Please note that these websites will charge you a fee to list your room.

2- **Rent your property to holidaymakers:** If your house or flat is near a tourist attraction, a tube/train station or in a nice area, and you can vacate the house during the children's school holidays such as Easter, summer and half-term, then you should consider renting your house out to tourists. This is big business. In areas of London, house owners have been getting between £100 and £250 a night. Other areas in the north of England can get as much as £60 a night. You can even specify a minimum stay of say 5 or 14 days so that it is worth your while. Many websites help homeowners rent their homes to holidaymakers. Many of these holidaymakers are from Europe who prefers the 'personal' touch of a house in which they can cook their own food rather than overpriced and large corporate hotels. You should consider listing your property at one of the following websites: Airbnb.co.uk, Wimdu.com, Holidaylettings.co.uk or Homeaway.co.uk, but there are much more that you can find online. Please note that some charge a listing fee, while others will charge you nothing unless you rent after which they will charge you a processing fee. You can sign up with as many as you like and can afford.

3- **Rent your property out for film set:** If you lucky and there is a company looking for a location to film in your area, then you could be making good money there. Some websites suggest you can make as much as £2500 a day (Davidson, 2013). We never tried it but here are some links to websites that suggest this is possible: http://www.uklocations.co.uk/get-touch/, www.locationworks.com/register/, www.shootfactory.co.uk/register-location.html and many more.

Chapter 2: Mortgage Requirements

In this chapter we will explain some of the key financial requirements for applying for a mortgage. Why deposits are now a requirement for your application. We will also explain the different mortgage features and options that are found in the hope that this can help homeowners select the most appropriate option.

2.1: What is a Deposit?

A deposit is an essential requirement for banks to issue a mortgage. It is the buffer that banks need to protect them should the homeowner fail to pay over a period of time and consequently the banks have to repossess the property.

As mentioned in the previous chapter banks look for deposits of between 5% to 10% of the house price depending on the reason you want to buy, your income, and your finances. Keep in mind that they can ask as much as 50% deposit if they feel you do not have the right requirements. The bank does not take the deposit. The deposit is paid; along with the money, the homeowner borrows from the bank to the previous owner of the house. The deposit represents insurance for the bank should anything happen such that the borrower is not able to keep up with repayments and the bank, therefore, has to repossess the house. At one point during the housing boom of 2005-2008, some banks did not even ask for a deposit because they believed that there was no risk of losing any money even if they repossessed your home. In fact, some banks allowed homeowners to borrow 125% of the value of the property so that the homeowner could use the extra 25% to make improvements. This was a very big gamble. Not surprisingly, it is unlikely that banks will ever go back to lending in the same way they did during the boom of the late 2000s.

2.2: How do deposits work?

From homeowners' point of view, the deposit is the main loss they could incur should they fail to keep up their repayments. However, the process of repossession is a long process, and banks are not keen at all to take the property off the homeowner unless they have no other choice. Usually, banks issue warnings for the first three to six months, after which it takes is another three to six months to get the house repossessed by the courts. In the time the bank is reprocessing the house, the bank loses money on interest. What is more, because banks sell reprocessed properties in a hurry, banks also lose money on the value of the house.

The purpose of the deposit is to recover some of the bank's losses in case of a repossession. So when the whole process is finished, there is usually no money left from the owner's deposit. During the boom of the housing market when house prices were going up so quickly, banks were so confident that they could recover their money they did not require a deposit.

Fact 10:

A deposit belongs to the homeowner and will be returned along with all the repayments the homeowner makes whenever they sell.

At the time of writing this book, December 2016, banks were requiring first-time homeowners to pay a minimum deposit of 5%, previous homeowners 10% and investors buying to let (to rent out) a 20% deposit.

Bigger deposits may be required in some circumstances such as when the homeowner has a very poor credit history, has been rejected by other banks, or because they have a shortfall in what they are allowed to borrow. Take, for example, a homeowner who can borrow a maximum of £150,000 but wants to buy a house that is £200,000. The bank will let them buy that house, but they will need to find a deposit of £50,000 to cover the difference. The £50,000 in this instance represents 25% of the value of the house, and for the bank, this is a bigger buffer, and hence they will be more than happy to approve the mortgage.

2.3: How to protect the deposit

The homeowner's deposit and subsequent repayments represent an investment that should be protected. This is your money in the form of 'bricks' in your home.

The deposit and subsequent repayments are the equity (see Chapter One) that the homeowner builds into the house. In the event of unexpected problems, the homeowner should act quickly to defend their investment. At the end of Chapter One, we provided a variety of solutions to almost every possible problem a homeowner can face. The key problem concerning most homeowners is the fear of losing their jobs. In this event, let's emphasise an important fact which does not apply in many other countries, in the UK even if a homeowner loses their job they are able to protect their home and their investment. Provided they are a UK or EU citizen and have been paying taxes; the Job Centre will protect their home. The Job Seeker Centre, the place where people in the UK go to sign on as being unemployed and to get support, will usually be more than happy to arrange payment of the interest on a mortgage. The Job Seeker Centre will also issue the homeowner with papers that will force or request from the bank to stop demanding the full repayment on the house. Some banks will be happy to maintain this arrangement for a year or even longer. From the banks' perspective, they are not losing anything. The money they have invested is still generating interest. The only difference is that now the homeowner is not paying off their mortgage that means they will probably take longer to pay it off. This is not a problem for the bank because of many banks issue 'interest-only mortgages', so this is no different.

So let us take a homeowner with property bought for £180,000, a £155,000 mortgage, a £25,000 deposit, an interest rate of 5% and repayments of 30 years. Their mortgage is £832 a month.

However, after 5 years the homeowner finds themselves without a job. The Job Centre will ask them to get a letter from the bank which details the 'interest only' payment; the bank will state that the interest-only payment is £594 a month. The Job Centre will pay that amount to the bank and request that the bank stop demanding the remaining £238 until the homeowner finds a job. The months and years during which the homeowner does not have a job will not cost the bank anything, the homeowner will not lose their home, and the equity is protected, but it will mean that it will take the homeowner longer to own the house. In the scheme of things, this is not a very bad situation.

Fact 11:

On a repayment mortgage, every monthly payment includes two parts: the interest part and the repayment part.

2.4: Where to get a deposit if you don't have one?

The best way to get a deposit is by saving it. It could be very hard to save money when a big chunk of your income is being swallowed up by rent. But trying to tighten belts and missing one or two holidays for the sake of starting to own your own house is definitely worthwhile. Even if you cannot save the whole amount but a good portion of it, then you could consider other ways to top up your deposit.

Selling valuables:

Consider a high-value non-essential item that you may have: a car, if public transport is a feasible option for a while, jewellery, expensive watches and electrical items. It is worth considering anything that could top up your deposit and which you could buy again once you have established yourself and own a house.

Borrow from family/friends

It may sound too obvious to some people. However to others, it is not so obvious. If it is possible to borrow some money from family or friends with a pledge to pay them back in a year or two, then this could be a way forward. Consider the savings from the rent and the fact that the money you are borrowing will be yours in the form of a house deposit anyways. In a year or two, you may be able to borrow money much more easily because you are a house owner with a good credit history. You will then be able to borrow that money from any bank, not necessarily your mortgage bank, and pay back your family and friends.

Loan/Credit card

If none of the above options is available, then you really do not have many choices. One option, which we do not recommend because it is risky but has been used in the past successfully, is to borrow the deposit. This option may sound ridiculous, but some people have made it work. If you get a loan from bank 'A', let's say for £10,000, it can easily go as a deposit for a mortgage to bank 'B'.

In theory, bank 'B' does not carry much risk. Bank 'B' gets the deposit it needs to protect its investment, even if the money has come from bank 'A'. Here is why it is risky though. Bank 'A' will not lend you the money if they know you are going to use this as a deposit. However, they will be more than happy to lend you the money if it is borrowed for a car, home improvements or other items. The loan is unsecured and tends to be at a higher interest rate of 6% to 10%, depending on your credit history. Bank 'B' will not be very happy to know that you borrowed that money to buy the house even though they had nothing to do with the loan. Bank 'B' would not want you to borrow money to use as a deposit because they do not want to encourage people to do it. Technically, however, it is legal because once you get a loan approved or you take money, you can do anything you want with it. There are issues with the fact that your intentions were not honest and that in some very rare cases banks could investigate if you do not manage to keep up your repayments. Our advice here is that you could use this option if you are short by a little amount. Let's say you need a £15,000 deposit and you only have £12,000. Why not borrow the additional £3,000 from your credit card or take out a loan to cover the shortfall.

2.5: Income

Your income can come from a variety of sources; do not just focus on the one main source as your only source. All sources of regular and non-regular income are considered when you apply for a mortgage. Having a clear understanding of what you can and cannot claim, as income is very important. Especially if you are self-employed, there are things that you must present to the bank as sources of income. Please note that while some banks may consider income from abroad, the majority will only consider income you generate in the UK.

2.5.1: Employment

If you have a full time or part-time employment with a company in the UK, then you will get payslips at the end of each month. Banks are very interested in income generated from contract employment. Provided you have the deposit, a reasonable credit history (we will talk about that in the next chapter), then all banks usually ask for is your pay slips as evidence of your income. Some banks require evidence of a three month's sequence of income, others require six months, and a few may ask for a year's worth of pay slips, especially if your income is not fixed from one month to another. In theory, you can buy your first house as early as three months after you get a fixed job. In fact, this is exactly what one of the authors of this book did. As soon as he got his third payslip and deposit, he applied for and purchased his first home.

Fact 12:

There are serious risks associated with taking out a mortgage that you cannot afford. The checks made by most banks are intended to protect you.

2.5.2: Self-employment

If you are self-employed, this means you generate your income from running your own business or running your own trade. Then it is a bit more complicated to prove your income but does not let this put you off. From the bank's point of view, anything you claim as income is hard to prove as you do not have payslips and sometimes little evidence to show in bank statements. Add to that; there is no fixed contract that tells the bank that your job is secured. However, there are several things you need to do to get the bank to lend you money. You will need to plan these carefully. First, you should consider getting all your customers to pay you via your bank account; direct bank transfers for large amounts and via card payment machine if you have many small payments.

If you receive cash payments, you will need to put them through your bank as well. This is step one. Step two is to pay your tax and ensure you get tax return evidence from the UK. This is HMRC Tax return. More information on how to do it can be found here: https://www.gov.uk/set-up-sole-trader. However, as an alternative, you could hire a tax return expert and ensure that he/she calculates your taxes correctly. These experts tend to charge anything between £50 and £500 depending on how complicated the financial transactions you make. Do not be put off by their fees. Tax return experts often know ways to reduce your tax bill without having to declare less income. There are many tax breaks for married couples, costs of starting a business and pension savings that you might not be aware of but which could reduce your tax bill. Details of these could fill an entire book on their own. The report of income and tax paid to HRMC will be checked by the banks and will be used to determine what they consider to be the maximum amount you can afford. They consider tax returns a reliable source of information because people do not 'overstate' their income when reporting their taxes.

2.5.3: Income and Risks

There have been many occasions where people have tried to lie in order to get a bigger mortgage or better rate. Our advice is that you should not lie but be sure that you can afford your mortgage.

All too often it is the people who falsify documents, make unsubstantiated claims, and under report their expenses that end up in financial difficulty when they cannot afford to pay their mortgage. If the bank believes you falsified your income, you could be considered criminal and lose the house and even go to prison. This is quite different from a situation where your financial circumstances have changed, or your employment income changed. Banks can work with you and try to reduce your payments by either switching your mortgage to interest only or changing your package to pay over a longer period of time thus reducing your repayments. If your income goes up and down from time to time, then you need to consider a mortgage that allows you to overpay and underpay. These are the issues you need to consider here.

2.6: Expenses involved in buying a property

On top of planning for the deposit, there are a few things a homeowner needs to plan for as expenses.

2.6.1: A Lawyer

A homeowner has to pay the expenses for a lawyer, which is usually from £500 to £3000 depending on how expensive the property is and how complicated the purchase is. On average, homeowners pay around £1000 to lawyers. Some lawyers will even offer you a capped or fixed cost, which means the cost, will not go up however long or complicated the process turns out to be. In the past, some mortgage companies, as a way to help you, offered to pay the lawyer's fees or just added that to your mortgage so you would not have to find the money upfront. If you find a bank that does that, then we recommend them. Also if this is your first mortgage, we strongly suggest you go through the estate agent's recommended lawyers as they tend to be more serious and give you a priority.

2.6.2: Land Registry Tax Duty

The land duty tax for England, Wales, and Northern Ireland has changed as of 22nd of November 2017; first time buyers get tax relief on buying a property less than £500.000. If you are not a first-time property buyer, properties over the value of £125,000 are subject to tax, which is called 'Stand Duty Land Tax' or SDLT for short. The tax office summarises this as follows:
- Nothing on the first £125,000 of the property price
- 2% on anything over £125,000 to £250,000.
- 5% on anything over £250.000 to £925.000.
- 10% on anything over £925,000 to £1.5 million
- 12% on anything over (above £1.5 million)

But you would be forgiven to assume a property valued at £126,000 has pay 2% tax – No it does not. You pay 2% on the £1000 extra, which comes up to just £20. If you find a house for £150,000, you pay 2% on £25,000 only, and this works out £500. If you want to buy a house for £200,000, you pay 2% on the £75,000 extra, which comes up to £1500.

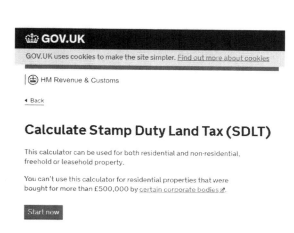

Figure 2.1 shows what online calculator provided to you by the tax office to help you calculate what your tax duty will be. You can find it at: www.hmrc.gov.uk/tool s/sdlt/land-and-property.htm

Figure 2.1 (HMRC, 2018)

As of 1st of April 2015, buying a home in Scotland follows a slightly different tax brackets to the ones listed in England, Wales, and Northern Ireland. In Scotland, the tax for buying property is called: "Land and Building Transaction Tax" or (LBTT). The following tax brackets are used:

- Nothing on first £135,000, of property price

- 2% on anything over £135,001 to £250,000

- 5% on anything over £250,001 to £325,000

- 10% on anything over £325,001 to £1 million.

- 12% on anything over £1 million.

The LBTT is slightly different; it starts taxing at £125,000 as opposed to £125,000 in other parts of the UK. The LBTT starts taxing higher rates for expensive properties. If you are looking to buy a property in Scotland, this online calculator by the Revenue Scotland will help you see what tax you will be asked to pay. https://www.revenue.scot/land-buildings-transaction-tax/tax-calculator/lbtt-property-transactions-calculator

In recent year, the UK government introduced a new tax to try to cool the property market including a higher tax for second homes set at 3% above whatever scale the property falls into and as long as the property costs more than £40,000.

Fact 13:

Expenses associated with buying a house can be anything between £1000 and £4000. Check, as some banks would be happy to include these costs in the mortgage, so you do not have to pay them up front.

2.6.3: Bank Charges

There may also be a charge for processing your mortgage, which varies from one bank to another. Most banks will not charge any fees for processing your mortgage, while others may add the charge to the overall mortgage so you pay it over a long period of time. For example, when taking out a mortgage for £52,000 a bank charged one of the authors £1000 in processing fees. This may seem like quite a lot, but the interest rate was 4.2%, lower than the average of 5.2% and the author determined that in the long run, the processing fees were worth paying for the sake of a lower rate.

Furthermore, the author did not have to pay the processing fees up front because the bank just added them to the overall cost, so his mortgage on the property was £53,000 over a period of 30 years. Of course, we all want a bank that does not charge us any fees. However, the ones that do not charge us any fees may not be necessarily offering the best value because they will need to make their money in other ways.

2.7: Types of mortgages

There are many types of mortgage that you could choose from. When the time arrives, and you find your first house, speak to the bank, and they will tell you about the options they have. The simplest and most common two have already been introduced in this book: Repayment and Interest-Only mortgages. We also explained the Flexible mortgage, which is a type of a Repayment mortgage. You can skip this section if you have decided that the type of mortgage you want is one of these. However, if you are still unsure, read on. We will go over these mortgages again and discuss some of the more complex types and their associated advantages and disadvantages.

2.7.1: Repayment Mortgages

This represents the most common mortgage for first-time buyers and homeowners in the UK. It is also not difficult to understand.

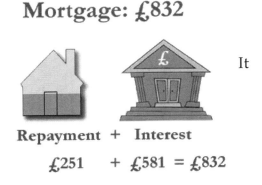

Mortgage: £832

Repayment + Interest

£251 + £581 = £832

Diagram 2.1: Repayment Mortgage.

You borrow money over a long period of time. Every month when you make your regular payment, a portion of that money goes to pay the interest while another portion goes to pay part of the loan. See diagram 2.1. Over the period of the mortgage, you start to accumulate equity in the house. There are three main types of repayment mortgage: fixed mortgages, variable mortgages and flexible mortgages.

2.7.2: Fixed mortgages

The repayments are fixed. The bank agrees a fixed rate for you from the start. Usually, a fixed rate mortgage is fixed for two, three, four or five years. So if you agree to a fixed rate of 5.2% for five years, this means whatever happens in the money market, your repayments will not change.

With a fixed repayment mortgage, your monthly mortgage becomes like your fixed rent contract. However, here you can have it fixed for up to five years. There is usually a penalty of £250 - £1000 if you decide to close, move, or change your mortgage during the fixed contract period but the security and savings you get over the period of the mortgage sometimes make it worthwhile.

2.7.3: Variable mortgages

The repayments may change. The bank will usually link the interest you pay to the Bank of England's interest rate or the bank's own lending interest rate which is also called the Standard Variable Rate (SVR). There are some occasions where you can be lucky and get amazing deals here, but there are risks as well. One of the authors of this book gambled in 2008 when he took a variable mortgage, anticipating that the Bank of England would drop its rate. The deal he got was 0.4% above the Bank of England's interest rate, which at the time was 5.0%.

For a few months, the author paid 5.4% or £870 a month on a property which would have cost £1000 a month to rent anyways, so he saw the benefits anyway. This was a good deal and shortly afterwards, and as had been anticipated, the Bank of England rate started going down to help the economy recovers. Within a year, the rate of Bank of England rate went down to 0.5% and remained so for the last four years. The author has been paying an interest rate of 0.9% or £500 a month, making a saving of £35,520 in the last eight years whilst living in a property he owns at the cost of half the rent. It is important here to emphasise that there is usually a risk with these variable mortgages because interest rates could go up as well as down. With the Brexit vote, the market is expected to be unpredictable. But this should not put you off. Do your research and seek financial advisors' opinion. Bank of England rate of 0.25% is unlikely to go lower. So this may not be the best time to go with a variable rate.

In fact, at the time of writing this book, there have been clear indications that Bank of England is about to raise its interest rates, given that the economy is doing better than expected. Variable mortgages are, therefore, no longer the best choice.

Fact 14:

Variable mortgages almost always appear cheaper than fixed mortgages. This is because there is a risk with variable mortgages that the interest rate may go up.

2.7.4: Flexible mortgages

This is a type of repayment mortgage. If your income varies from time to time, then a flexible mortgage should be your choice. With the previous types of mortgage, some banks will not allow you to over pay, and those that do will just reduce the number of years until you finish paying your mortgage rather than actually reducing the amount you pay each month. Flexible mortgages allows the homeowner to over pay so if there are occasions when you are not earning as much money as you usually do, the bank will use money from the overpayments. Many banks will be happy to offer it as an option. Whilst you could have a flexible mortgage with a fixed or variable interest rate, if you do not want to take too many risks then you are better off with a Flexible Fixed rate.

2.7.5: Joint mortgages

Sometimes one person's income is not enough to obtain enough mortgage for the house they want. If two people work in the house, then they could buy the house jointly.
Joint mortgages can be taken out with a partner, with a friend living with you or a colleague. This option is especially popular in densely populated areas of London where rents are very high, and a mortgage works out cheaper provided that payment is shared by two people. This option is also very popular with married or civil partnership couples where both work and they need a bigger place. Joint mortgages make life a bit easier as each partner pays part of the deposit, expenses and mortgage payments. However, joint mortgages are a bit more complex because the banks will need to check the income and credit history of both owners. Joint mortgages can be repayment mortgages or any of their three sub-types. Joint mortgages can be interest only, buy-to-let, or any of the other types. The only key thing here is that the mortgage is shared.

2.7.6: Interest-only mortgages

Mortgage: £581

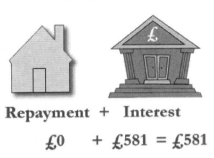

Repayment + Interest

£0   + £581 = £581

Diagram 2.2: Interest-Only Mortgage.

As the bank's main income is the interest that it makes from the homeowner's mortgage, what the homeowner does with the house - sell it, keep it, pay it off, or not pay it off - does not really make a huge difference to the bank. This is why many banks offer interest-only mortgages. These mortgages do not tend to have an end date. You can live in your house for two years or fifty years. All you are doing is paying the interest. You do not own any part of the house other than what you put down as a deposit or what you accumulated as a result of an increase in the value of the house. If the value of the house goes up then, in theory, you make money as well. The only difference is that when you pay your monthly payment, you are only paying interest and no repayments. In other words, this mortgage has no equity repayment, just pure interest that will be significantly lower than the cost of renting, see diagram 2.2.

Some people use this type of mortgage to improve their credit history until they get a better interest rate, thereby paying less for their house. The obvious drawback of this type of mortgage is that the mortgage is never paid off and hence, the house would never be owned by the borrower. So basically, you have gone back to renting. Some people are more than happy to take this option because, as we saw in our earlier examples, the interest-only is many times less than half the rent and this helps you build a good saving.

To calculate interest rate:

Banks calculate interest using Annual Percentage Rate (ARP), which means that every interest payment is calculated on annual bases then divided by 12, each and every month. So if a bank says the interest is 5.2% on a £150,000 will have the interest to pay the bank as £150,000 x (5.2÷100)= £7,800 over the year. They then divide it over 12 months (£7,800÷12) = £650.00.

2.7.7: Buy-to-let mortgages

A buy-to-let mortgage means the property is bought with a mortgage for the purpose of renting it out to people. This is a bit more risky for the bank and the owner. A higher rate of repossessions of buy-to-let properties takes place compared to homeowners' properties. This is mainly because of the risks that some investors take in buying too many properties. Once they stumble on one or more bad tenants who do not pay their rents, they get into financial trouble and lose everything. First of all, the deposit on this mortgage type is not 5% to 10%, but 20%. A buy-to-let property is harder to get and banks usually perform extra checks on your affordability including the level of rent you might be able to charge for the property. The author who bought a flat in Scotland had to prove that the rent he could charge was £550 and the mortgage £265 in order to secure the buy-to-let mortgage. Proof of these figures was in addition to all the other checks. The government is also putting an additional cost on these types of purchases to discourage them. The government cancelled tax relief on mortgage interest payments. Now investors have to pay tax on the income, not the profit. Someone with a £150,000 buy-to-let mortgage on a property worth £200,000, with a monthly rent of £800, in the past, would have a net profit of around £2,160 a year. Under the new system, the net profit would drop to £960. The cancelling of tax relief only affects investors who do buy-to-let using a mortgage. This does not affect those who invest by buying the property outright. Another measure the government introduced is that buy-to-let properties and the second house would incur an extra 3 percent stamp duty (tax) when purchasing.

These are good news for first-time buyers like you; it will mean less competition from amateur and risk-taking buy-to-let investors.

2.7.8: Other types of mortgages:

These are less popular, but you may come across them: Discount variable, Tracker, Offset and Capped mortgages. We generally do not recommend any of these options as they tend to be riskier. We will now explain why.

Fact 15:

There are many mortgages and options within mortgages. Cheaper mortgages are almost always associated with more risk such as a change in interest rates. We strongly recommend you make your affordability plans around a repayment mortgage.

Discounted variable mortgages: This usually involves an offer whereby the bank provides you with a mortgage that is at a discounted rate compared to their Standard Variable Rate (SVR). This discount will be for a limited time of a few months up to two years, after which the rate goes back to the bank's standard rate. You should be careful as this is not always the best choice because there are usually high processing costs associated with this type of mortgage which very much offsets whatever saving you might have made.

Tracker mortgages: These are very similar to variable mortgages. However, the tracking rate is usually low at the start of the mortgage but then goes up. For instance, many of the variable rates at the time of writing this book were 2.5% above the Bank of England rate, making the rate of borrowing for a homeowner 2.75% (because the Bank of England rate is 0.25%). A Tracker mortgage would give you an initial offer of say 1% above the Bank of England for two years, and after that, it goes up to 2.5%. What banks are doing here is giving you easier payment options for the first few months and years. Again they seem to offset this with higher rates later or by charging you very high processing fees.

Offset mortgages: When you have savings in your bank account, at the end of the month that money can be used to 'offset' part of your mortgage cost. This may sound bizarre, and it is bizarre. You may wonder who would actually borrow money for mortgage if they have a considerable savings. Well some people do. The idea is that if you think you will be saving a lot, provided you have an offset mortgage then you can put those savings into the same bank with which you have your mortgage. In return, the bank will not charge you interest. For example, let's say you have a mortgage of £155,000, an interest rate of 5%, and savings of £24,000.

Provided you have an offset mortgage then you will only be paying interest on £131,000, and your repayments could go down by £1200 a year or £100 less a month. This will only happen if the bank matches the same rate and hence you need to check that. But you may rightly ask: "Why not pay the £24,000 against the mortgage in the first place?" Well, this is a very good question. But if you ever need money for urgent work, a wedding, or something else perhaps unexpected then you will need to ask for a loan, and that will be at a much higher interest rate. This option is selected by people who have savings but who may need to use them at short notice.

Capped mortgages: This is a type of variable mortgage, which provides some protection for the buyer. The bank will assure the homeowner that the mortgage will never exceed a certain rate whatever the level of UK interest rates in general. There may also be a limit as to how low the rate can go. Like some other types of mortgage, you may find that this option comes with processing costs. Furthermore, the variable rates will be higher than the standard variable. So, for instance, while the normal variable rate could be 2.5% above the Bank of England rate, the variable capped mortgage rate may be capped at 6% but would start with a variable rate of 3.5% above the Bank of England rate.

Mortgage Advice Bureau, 2014

2.8: Help To Buy Schemes

There are quite a few "help to buy" schemes open to both British and EU citizens living in the UK. Some schemes are even open to non-UK and EU citizens so please check with the providers. There are many help to buy schemes available, and they can change rapidly. We will be listing some of the most popular schemes, explaining the advantages and disadvantages, and identifying the types of people to whom such schemes are ideally suited. Because there are so many schemes, we recommend you double check with the mortgage advisors at your estate agent the latest schemes and the ones which best match your needs. Here are some of the popular help to buy schemes that were operating at the time this book was published.

2.8.1: Shared Ownership

As we said before, mortgage providers are only interested in making sure that they have a 'deposit' buffer to protect them should you fail to pay. How you manage to get the deposit is not so important as long as it is legal. Housing associations and builders provide one of the schemes that have been extremely popular known as Part-buy scheme. They sell you a percentage of the house and then rent you another percentage at a low rate. Because you are borrowing far less than the value of the house or flat, you only need to provide a small deposit for the bank. For example, say you want to buy a property that costs £100,000. A 10% deposit needed means you have to find £10,000 and borrow £90,000 from the bank. However, with shared ownership of say 50% with the builder, you only have to borrow £45,000 from the bank. You would only need to find a £5,000 deposit and you could rent the other 50% of the property from the builder/housing association for a low price. Some builders or housing associations may even pay your deposit.

The advantages of this scheme are that it helps you if you cannot borrow a lot because banks can only lend you up to four times your income. It can also help you if you cannot get the deposit ready. At later stages, and when your repayments are firmly established, you can buy a larger percentage of your property.

The disadvantages of this scheme are that it tends to be associated with newly built properties, which are typically over-priced by 10% to 20%. You may also have problems selling the property if you do not own all of it since few people like the idea of half owning property, the other half of which is rented but is controlled by a builder or housing association. For instance, you may not be allowed to rent the property without the explicit permission of the builder or housing association. Our advice would be to choose this option only if the combination of mortgage and rent is less than what the full rent would have been and you intend to live for a very long time in that house. So in time, you will own it while paying less to live there. It will also make sense to choose this option if you intend to buy the remaining percentage of the property within few years.

2.8.2: Government "Help To Buy" Schemes:

The UK government has been coming up with several schemes to help new buyers to get on the property ladder and existing buyers to upgrade. Here is the latest help to buy schemes: Equity Loan, Help to Buy ISA, London Help to Buy, and Mortgage Guarantee scheme.

2.8.2.1. Loan Equity Scheme.

Used to be called "The Affordable Homeownership Scheme". This scheme helps first time buyers or homeowner wishing to buy new build properties for up to £600,000. The scheme works as follows: The Government pays 20% of the equity of the house, charges you nothing for the first five years and very little after that until you pay the government back their deposit. For instance, say you find a newly built house for £200,000, and the bank requires you to pay a 5% deposit.

If you buy the property with the "Affordable Homeownership scheme" you will have to pay a £10,000 deposit, the Government will lend you £40,000, and you get a mortgage from the bank for £150,000.

As far as the banks are concerned, beyond your 5% deposit, there is no additional risk of a further 20% of the property. The banks' risk is very low, and hence they can offer you cheaper rates.

The advantages of this scheme are that you will be borrowing less and paying less in mortgage payments for at least five years. Even after five years, you still pay far less than a full mortgage.

The disadvantages of this scheme are that you are forced to buy new homes, which tend to be 10% to 20% more expensive than the market value. Also, you must pay the Government's loan within 25 years.

Our advice is that you should choose this option if you are intent to buy a new home anyways. Sometimes you have no choice. For example, your preferred area may only consist of new houses. Alternatively, there may be certain constraints – you need a house near a school, your workplace, or particular transport links. Finally it could be that the maximum the banks can lend you is not enough and therefore this is your ideal option to upgrade to bigger house.

2.8.2.2. London Help to Buy Scheme:

To reflect the current property prices in London, the Government has increased the Equity Loan scheme's upper loan limit from 20% to 40% for buyers in all London boroughs. The London Equity Loan scheme could help homebuyers own their own home in the capital a bit easier. When the homeowner puts down as little as a 5% deposit on a newly built home, the Government equity loan will lend this homeowner as much as 40% of the value of the property. So let's say you find your first house in London for £200,000 and you want to use the London Equality Loan. You will only need £10,000 deposit. The government will lend you up to £80,000, and you only need to get a mortgage of £110,000. This does make it much easier to get a mortgage from the banks.

2.8.2.3. Help to Buy ISA:

If you have started saving to buy your first home, you will notice that the interest rates are quite poor at the moment. A scheme arranged with banks to help first-time buyers is called Help to Buy: ISA. The Government will boost your savings by 25%. So, for every £200 a homeowner saves, they will receive a government bonus of £50. The maximum government bonus you can receive is £6,000. So it is definitely worth checking with your bank. So if you target is to save £24,000, you could get faster with a "Help to Buy: ISA" as you will get there by the time you have saved £18,000. How does it work? To start your account, in your first month, you can deposit a lump sum of up to £1,200. Save up to £200 a month into the scheme. Once you get to £1,600, you will receive your first bonus of £400. And from there after, every month you save £200, you get £50 bonus. We strongly recommend this option if you are about to start saving for your deposit.

2.8.2.4. Mortgage Guarantee:

This scheme starts 1st of January 2017. The Help to Buy: mortgage guarantee scheme works in the same way as any other mortgage except that under the scheme the Government offers the banks a guarantee on the mortgage. Because of this support, the banks taking part will require homebuyers a smaller deposit. The homeowner will still be fully responsible for the mortgage repayments. This scheme is best explained in an example. Let's say you want a large mortgage of £200,000 and for whatever reason, the bank wants a 20% (£40,000) deposit. However, you only have 5% (£10,000). The bank will not lend you £190,000; this is a risky loan for them. Under this scheme, the government will guarantee a £30,000 of the loan. They will not pay it; they will just provide the bank with a 'guarantee' papers. If you fail to pay and the bank repossess the house and losses money, you will lose your deposit of £10,000 and the government will pay the bank for the part they guaranteed up to £30,000. All this scheme does is that it helps first time buyers purchase a house with smaller deposit and reduces the risk on the banks that are offering the loan.

All these schemes come with 'conditions'. Some of which is that you have to be a first time home buyer, do not own any other properties, and the property value does not exceed 4.5 times your income. Keep an eye on this, and other government offers as they change at short notice. This link is for England but also has links to similar schemes in Scotland, Wales, and Northern Ireland. Read more about this scheme at www.helptobuy.gov.uk.

2.8.3 The Key Workers Scheme and Private Schemes:

There are many private schemes that are run by builders in association with councils. In such schemes, builders who apply for planning permission will be asked by the local councils to allocate a percentage of their properties to key workers and other people who cannot afford to live in the area. The councils usually define what they consider to be key workers and these definitions change depending on the skills needed by these councils.

For instance, at the time of publishing this book, the Royal Borough of Greenwich promoted a scheme which defined key workers as those people working in the teachers, doctors, nurses, porters, social workers, firefighters, police, and many more. (see: http://www.royalgreenwich.gov.uk/info/200077/private_housing/513/low-cost_home_ownership)

Of course, check your council's website with an explanation as to who qualifies. Councils will provide links to these builders so that you can apply online. In some cases, the builder will set a date for homebuyers to queue for a chance to purchase an affordable property. These properties will not be the prime properties in the development but they would be sold at a significant discount, anything between 10% and 50%.

To take one example, a major building development in Greenwich and the builder agreed with the council to sell some 10% of the flats at a 30% discount. There was, of course, a set of criteria for people to apply but the builder set a date and did not specify how many flats would be released. People queued outside the gates of the development; some in tents overnight, and when the gates were opened the first 20 couples/families were able to purchase their flats at significantly lower prices. Finding out if your council operates this scheme is not too difficult. You can either search online using the words 'affordable houses' or 'key workers scheme' and the name of your council.

Alternatively, you can ring your council and ask them if there is a scheme operating at the moment. We recommend that anyone who is interested in purchasing a property this way should check at least once a month. You never know when such properties might come up. The availability of these types of property is typically advertised reasonably well in advance. Here are some of the council links we found at the time of writing this book:

Islington Council:
https://www.islington.gov.uk/housing/finding-a-home/housing-options-for-key-workers
Southwark Council:
http://www.2.southwark.gov.uk/info/200052/looking_for_a_home/971/different_types_of_housing/6
East Cambridge: http://www.eastcambs.gov.uk/housing/key-workers-housing-advice
Windsor Council:
https://www3.rbwm.gov.uk/info/200118/housing/119/shared_ownership/2
Tower Hamlets:
http://www.towerhamlets.gov.uk/lgnl/housing/lettings_and_the_housing_list/key_worker_scheme.aspx

Newham Council:
https://www.newham.gov.uk/Pages/Services/Renting-an-affordable-home.aspx
Edinburgh Council:
http://www.edinburgh.gov.uk/info/20124/new_council_hom
es/254/building_affordable_homes

You can find much more online.

Chapter

3

Chapter 3: Credit History

In this chapter we explore the underground world of financial checks carried out by banks and businesses, and we will see how it is easy for individuals to review their credit rating. We will also be making recommendations about how to improve a credit rating and what actions you should take to make sure your mortgage application is approved.

Credit history is held in databases in the United Kingdom for the purposes of tracking the financial activities of individuals. The source of this information tends to be three main credit-referencing agencies: Experian, CallCredit, and Equifax (Gunn, 2013). Any authorised organisations, such as banks, can access the data from credit history databases. Even the activity of 'checking' your credit history is recorded.

A record in the credit history database is created as soon as a person makes any financial transactions or other related procedures within the UK such as opening a bank account, applying for a credit card, payments through PayPal, gas/electricity accounts, mobile contracts and even non-payment related operations such as registering with a council. The credit history is kept for the duration of the life of the individual although some records are deleted after a period. From the credit history, financial institutions create a 'credit score'. The best way to think of a credit score is to compare it to your school report. The better you perform, the better your overall score will be. If you do not do well, your overall score will not be good, and some schools/colleges will not accept you when you apply. Similarly, your credit history is the record of how you 'financially behaved' as an individual when it comes to money. Also, like a school report, even if you did badly at one time, you can always work hard to improve it. And if you do really well, over time you can completely remove an old record and your credit score will go up.

As the credit history system has been in operation in the UK for a very long time, it has been adapted to keep track of all a person's financial transactions in one place even if changes occur to that person's details. It keeps track of things like changes of address, marriage, changes of bank accounts and others. The main reason why it has become possible for this system to work is that lots of so-called 'financial information' is collected whenever you perform financial transactions. For example, whenever a person tries to open a bank account or register for a credit card they must provide related details such as previous addresses in the last 5 years, previous surnames, employment details and more. The system, therefore, will be able to track that person, and the new details are added to their record.

Whatever your views about such a system and how the scoring system works, you should try to take advantage of it. Only then will you learn to love it. The system has been built in such a way as to allow the updating of your personal data even if you made some financial mistakes. Although you have to be careful, as each mistake or financial mismanagement will mean higher interest rates on your mortgage, credit cards, and loans, if you are a persistent offender, you will find that you will not be able to borrow anything.

3.1: Why is credit history important?

As mentioned earlier credit history can be accessed by any authorised organisation, but you can also access it yourself. For mortgage purposes, banks access a borrower's credit history to assess whether a loan can be issued and if so, what would be the best rate that they can offer. Banks rarely offer you a different product, as they tend to define their rate by a certain set of criteria. However, the better the borrower's credit history – the lower the interest rate you are able shop around for.

What contributes to a bad credit history? Many activities could contribute to a bad credit history. Activities such as not paying bills on time, not paying bills at all, criminal records, financial fraud, and other financial mismanagement will affect a borrower's credit history badly. A lot of data is stored in credit history databases especially data that relates to a borrower's court cases. By not paying bills, a borrower is actually damaging their credit history, which they may carry with them for life. Each lender assesses you in a different way and applies slightly different rates.

Usually, paying bills late three times leaves a very bad record in a credit history, and by ignoring a bill completely, a penalty mark is issued. This means that a potential borrower is considered unreliable. Having a good credit history, however, means that you can shop around for loans, credit cards and mortgages that are of a much lower interest rate. Compare this situation with someone with a very bad credit history forced to take out a payday loan at an interest rate of over 2,000% APR (Annual Percentage Rate). At the time of writing this book, a good credit history could lead to a loan at as low as 2% APR. The difference between a person with excellent credit history and one with a bad credit history is huge. The same principles apply to mortgage rates. If the homeowner does not have a very good credit history, mortgages could be issued but usually at a higher rate than to others with very good or excellent credit histories. At the time of publication, mortgage rates varied between 1.99% and around 8% APR. As a new homeowner, you may find that the only banks that will give you credit to buy are at the upper end of the rate. However, with time the rate gets better and better. With clever planning, you could obtain a rate that is surprisingly low. The author's mortgage at the time of publication stood at 0.9% APR, which is less than 1%! Not only that, he has been able to keep that rate for more than eight years. Although it will be very difficult to replicate this in the future, we will tell you in the next chapter how the author achieved such a low rate. Nevertheless, the rewards of having a great credit history are still significant.

3.2: How can you check your own credit history?

There are several companies in the UK that are able to check credit histories, and several will even give you a full report. One particular website, experian.com, is the most popular in the UK.

Experian.com usually offers the first month as a free trial, which gives you a chance to take full advantage of their services. Experian.com will undoubtedly ask you the same detailed questions that many banks will ask. They will then generate a report showing all the credit cards you have opened, loans issued in your name, addresses you lived in, report if you are paying your bills on time, your council records…etc. The website not only shows your credit history but also allows you to see mistakes or penalty marks recorded against you. In some cases, the website may be able to advise you how to fix these problems.

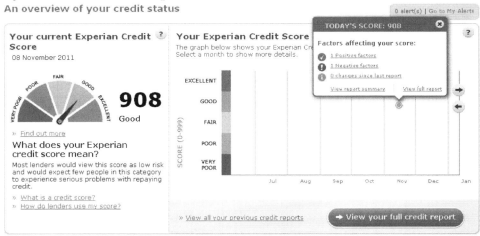

Figure 3.1. Example of Experian Credit Scoring and report. (Experian, 2014)

The other very important advantage of Experian and similar credit history websites is that they allow you to see your chances of getting a mortgage. As mentioned in earlier chapters, you have to make sure that your first mortgage is definitely going to be accepted. Otherwise, it makes applying for the next one more difficult and will probably cost you more in the form of higher rates. Applying for a mortgage when a company has declined you make other lending companies more cautious because they do not know why you got declined. In fact, you will find some banks asking you when applying: "Have you ever had a loan or mortgage application rejected?"

Therefore it is highly recommended that you use credit history websites or companies before you apply, as they will be able to tell you if you have a 'good' or 'very good' chance of getting a mortgage. Keep in mind that anything below 'good' will mean that your credit history has to be improved before you can apply for a mortgage. Sometimes the credit history companies will suggest the banks who might be willing to lend to you, which is why if you worried about your credit history you should use these credit history services before you apply for a mortgage. Even if you pay a small fee for these credit history services for a few months, as soon as your mortgage is approved, you could close your account with them.

We all want the lowest rate and why not! The difference between the upper and lower rate can be as much as £5,000 a year for a £100,000 mortgage – or £415 every month! However, you have to be realistic. It is unlikely that you will get a very low rate at first because banks do not trust you yet but there are things you could do to keep getting the lowest rate possible. Here are our suggestions. Never sign up for a fixed rate mortgage that is more than two years. Every two years when your contract finishes, shop around for the lowest rate. Even by ringing your own mortgage bank you may discover that they are happy to offer you a lower rate so you could stay with them. In the majority of cases, you will be able to get a better deal every year because your credit history will be improving as banks start to trust you more and more.

3.3: How to create a good credit history

Your credit history needs to be treated very seriously. It is a very valuable asset. It is extremely important that you do not exceed what you can afford. This does not mean that you should not get credit cards or loans. In fact it is important that you get at least two credit cards and/or a loan.

But what you need to do is to make sure that you always pay them on time, as this will help you build up a good credit history. The author got his credit card before his house and made sure that it was always paid on time – especially important since the interest rate on credit cards can be as much as 30% APR. But he knew that lending companies needed to see that he was able to manage his money. Showing that you have credit cards and that you always pay them on time, along with other bills, suggests to lenders that you can be trusted with money. The same principles that apply to credit cards apply to mortgages. Apply only to credit card companies that will accept you, bearing in mind that initially, it will be the ones with very high-interest rates. It is recommended that you get two to three credit cards but do not use them much, making sure they cover your general spending and that you pay them off by the end of the month, so you do not pay any interest on them. That is really the trick with credit cards; if you pay them by the end of the month, you do not pay any interest. Keep in mind that building credit history does not happen overnight. It takes from two to five years - two years if you keep it clean, and you get a steady job but up to five years if you do not make a good start. It is very important at this stage not to get into credit difficulties. You should never abuse credit cards or allow them to be misused. It is very easy to be caught up in debt or be tempted to let someone abuse your cards. This will damage your credit history. This is why credit cards are like a 'mini' test of how you can manage a much bigger loan such as a mortgage. Many people, especially those who come from abroad, think that changing some details will delete their history. At best, it may start a new history, but banks tend to track you through your transactions and your council records.

Even people who, in the past, thought that they could abuse all their credit cards and then run away to another country are discovering that they can still be traced by credit card companies (Uren, 2013). However, by paying all your debts and bills on time, you will start getting a green mark against your credit history and thereby build

---

Fact 16:

Having a bad credit history does not mean you cannot get a mortgage. It will be difficult and you will end up paying more interest. Ideally, you should work on clearing your history first.

---

and maintain an excellent credit history. With every payment missed on credit cards, telephone bills, mobile bills, electricity/gas bill, council tax and other bills, a red mark is recorded against your history. This stays on your record for years.

3.4: Creating and recovering credit history

To build up a good credit history or fix a poor one, credit history websites such as experian.com are recommended. Sometimes a few actions can be done to improve a credit rating, but these things can take time. If you have been in the UK for two years or more, you should join Experian or any other financial credit history website and read their report on your credit history. Keep in mind that it may take between 2 to 5 years to build a good credit history. Also, it is important to know that a record will remain in your credit history for a long time, whether it has been fixed or not. Credit companies tend to care more about recent credit history unless there are very serious issues such as criminal convictions, financial fraud or declarations of bankruptcy. Such issues are very damaging on anyone's records and can really prevent you from getting a mortgage. To build good credit history, getting credit cards and loans is important. Many people rightly refuse to get a credit card because credit cards can be expensive. However, if you pay off the balance at the end of each month, then you pay zero interest.

For example, the author has about eight credit cards and only uses two: American Express (because they give you cash back) and Barclaycard Visa (because it is accepted in many places). However the author always pays off the balance at the end of each month and has rarely ever paid any interest. Collectively, his credit cards provide him as much as £55,000 of credit, but he does not use them. By keeping these credit cards, he is able to show banks that he is trusted with money. Therefore credit cards, along with other financial transactions, are a cheap way to build a great credit history. If you have a poor credit history, then your individual circumstances will be such that it is nearly impossible for the authors of this book to advise you. You need to register with the credit history websites and follow their advice about how to either remove those red marks or improve your credit history despite these red marks.

You need to appreciate that many people have had terrible credit histories but were able to clear them in time. Banks and loan companies had an interest in loaning you money and provided that you prove yourself, they will do so. Keep in mind that if your credit history is poor, you could still apply for a mortgage using your partner's name.

Chapter 4: Searching for Properties in the UK

In this chapter we review the tools and techniques that help homeowners find the best deals and most appropriate locations to buy their property. We also provide tips on what the homeowner can do to get the lowest price possible by means of soft bartering.

T he way to find the ideal property to buy in the UK could be very different to the way you imagined. There are tools available for homebuyers to make sure that the price they see is not excessive or intended to cheat them out of their money. What is more, there are website tools that will make sure that you know what the 'estimated' value of the property that you are about to buy as well as what price the person who bought the house has paid.

Whilst we explain these tools from the following websites, we are only recommending them because they are the most popular at the time of writing this book. We recommend you also double check with your estate agent if they know of alternative tools.

4.1: Searching websites/Apps for properties:

Some property websites and apps are the easiest and fastest way to find properties and to develop a good understanding of the current values of properties in a certain area. It is our opinion that websites/apps are much better than searching via the windows of estate agents. The properties listed in the windows of estate agents could be old and intentionally made to look cheaper to get you to sign with them. The estate agents may be 'pushing' certain properties because they receive a higher commission or they may only cover one area of the city. Websites/apps give you the flexibility of searching on a much larger scale and are much more open, allowing you to see all your options. Estate agents fulfil a very important role that you will see later.

There are a few important things you need to think about as far as searching is concerned. Your initial location is obviously important. Bear in mind that you may have to extend your search to find cheaper or more accommodating places. You also need to consider the following:

1- **A number of rooms:** How many rooms do you want? Of course the more rooms you want, the more expensive it will be. The pictures and room descriptions are very important. In some city centres, the second room may be no bigger than a single bed.

2- **Type of property:** What type of property do you need? Here it gets challenging, and you may want to keep an open mind about your options.

    a. **Flats:** Most of the times you will find flats are cheaper, but they are cheaper for a reason. Flats tend to be noisier and attract a service charge that could be a lot of money - something that you do not need to deal with if you buy a house. Flats in England and Wales are likely to have a 'leasehold' agreement associated with the property. 'Leasehold' means that you will own the property for a certain number of years only. Usually, it is for 99 years unless every few years you renew the lease for a total of 99 years. If the flat or property you are about to buy is sold as leasehold, you need to check how many years are left on the leasehold and if you can renew it for a large number of years before you buy it. You should also ask how much it would cost to renew it. The risk, unlikely but not impossible, is that if you do not renew the leasehold for more than 30 years, then it would become expensive to renew. In the unlikely event, you never renew it then in 99 years the property will go back to the landlord that is usually a managing company. However, flats have their advantage. Size for size, flats are cheaper to buy, and the cost of repairs are shared which is where the service charge comes in. Also look out for the term 'studio' flat which means that the flat has an open kitchen in the living room – a modern design but a saving on space from a construction point of view.

Leasehold verses Freehold

Freehold means you own the property (bricks and land). With the right planning permissions, you can do anything to your property. Leasehold means, in theory, you own the bricks, but you rent the land. A property management company would usually manage the land, make repairs, and maintain communal gardens and car parks for an annual fee called a 'service charge'. Leasehold flats are very common in England and Wales but not in Scotland. Flats in Scotland are sold as freehold, and the flat owners work together to pay for any repairs and to manage their facilities. For more information, check the UK Government website at www.gov.uk/leasehold-property

b. **Houses:** You will find three types of Houses: The first type of house is listed as 'End of Terrace' that means the end of a row of houses. End of Terrace houses tends to be 10% to 20% more expensive because they tend to be quieter with fewer walls shared with the neighbours. Also, they tend to be slightly bigger. The second type 'mid-Terrace' means in the middle of a row of houses. Mid-terrace houses tend to be slightly cheaper because they share walls with neighbours on both sides but this issue is becoming less of a problem than in the past. One reason is that new buildings have much better sound insulation. Mid-terrace houses also have the added advantage of shared walls that means lower heating bills. Finally, you will find 'detached houses', which mean that they are separated from all the other houses. These houses can be between 20% and 30% more expensive than mid-terrace houses because they are completely detached from any other house. Gives you lots of privacy and peace but do expect the heating bills to be significantly higher.

c. **Bungalows:** In the UK, 'Bungalow' is a description given to a house that is compromised of one level, so there is no second floor. They tend to be built this way to accommodate elderly or disabled people. Because they tend to take more land space bungalows, cost more.

d. **Part-buy:** Finally you will find properties listed as part-buy or help to buy. These tend to be new properties where the construction company will 'part' sell you the house (25%, 50%, or 75%) but will own the remainder. This makes getting a mortgage much easier as you would need a much smaller deposit and mortgage. However, nothing is for free. The construction company will charge you 'rent' for the part you do not own until you pay it off. The philosophy here was that you would not be pressured to buy that percentage of the house until you are ready. You can, in fact, sell your share at any point to any potential buyer although you will find many buyers are not sure about part buying and part-renting. Our advice is not to choose this option unless all other doors are closed, and you believe you will live in the property until you pay it off in full. You can read more about this option in chapter 2.

3- **Distance:** You may specify a location, address, station or postcode but you will find most websites/apps will allow you to specify how far you are willing to extend your search. For instance, ¼ of a mile, ½ a mile, 1 mile, 2 miles...etc. Of course the more you extend your search, the more likely you are to find an inexpensive property that you can afford to buy in that area. However, cheaper does not always mean better as we will explain later.

4- **Auctioned properties:** Some websites/apps allow you to search for properties about to be sold in auctions. These tend to be listed very cheaply, but the advertised price may end up being different from the selling price. These properties tend to be sold at public auctions. In almost all cases they are sold at a lower price than the market price that makes them a bargain. But there are several catches. Firstly, unlike a standard purchase, these houses are sold "as is" which in English means "at your own risk". If there are serious problems with the property, it will be your responsibility to fix them. Also, on winning the bid you have to pay a deposit immediately, which is usually 10%, and you have to be able to pay it that day, in cash or by card. Furthermore, in many of these auctions, you have to complete the purchase within a certain number of days, usually around 28 days. If you do not complete within that time frame, you will lose your deposit, and you may be liable for the fees and charges to re-list the property. It is by no means a smart gamble unless you have money in the bank and have the resources to pay for it. Keep in mind that you will likely to have to pay some additional costs to upgrade the house or to fix it. There is normally a reason why a property would be auctioned, and that is because there must have been some issues associated with it. Banks try to sell these properties off first at a discount via estate agents. If such a repossessed property does not sell or the owner is in a hurry, then and only then do the banks go to auction.

5- **Repossessed properties:** These properties are difficult to spot on websites/apps because they are listed as normal properties. The clues are usually in the pictures and what the estate agents write. The first clues you will usually see are the pictures of the kitchen containing taps covered with white tape and the toilet tap and seat also covered with a white tap. The second clue can be found in what the estate agent writes in the listing. Phrases like 'we have been instructed by our 'client'…. 'gas and electricity cut off'…'central heating untested'…'deadline for offers.' Any of these tend to indicate that the property is repossessed. These properties tend to be sold at a discounted price, as banks want to sell them to get their money back. The banks are not after making a profit. What is more, you are likely to get accepted an offer to buy at 10% cheaper than the price listed if the bank does not get a higher offer before the deadline. Given that banks list the property in the first place at least 10% - 20% cheaper, this would be a good option to buy. You do not have to pay the deposit up front, only when you complete the purchase. You are not at risk of losing your deposit if your mortgage is not accepted. What is more, unlike auctioned properties, the banks can give you a reasonable amount of time to get your mortgage sorted. They do not tend to impose a 28-day deadline like many auctions require. The problem remains; if and when you can spot them, they may turn out to be a very good deal.

The following is a review of the three main sources of searching for websites in your area:

1- Rightmove.co.uk™:

Probably the most famous website in the UK for finding listed properties although the owners of Zoopla™ (the website we will talk about next) would strongly dispute that. Either way, we recommend you visit both Rightmove and Zoopla websites and apps because almost all estate agents list their properties in either one of these two and sometimes in both.

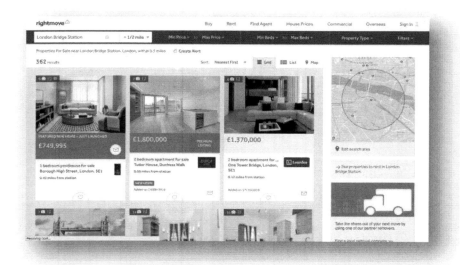

On visiting Rightmove, you will find a search engine that allows you to insert the name of the town, station, city, or postcode of the area you want.

The website initially will just list properties in that area, but then you have a chance on the left-hand side of the screen to make adjustments to your search. To specify how many rooms, type of property, distance, and type of buy of which you can narrow the search using the menu on the left-hand-side of the screen. This is where the information explained earlier will be very useful as now you know what it all means. You can also sort the list of properties so you can start from the cheapest property in that area all the way to the most expensive. This will always help as a means of starting your research and seeing what is happening sales wise in that area. The other tool that Rightmove provides is a better understanding of house values. This shows you at what prices houses were sold in the past in that area including the specific house.

Advanced options are available in Rightmove by opening an account. Opening one is free, and by drawing on a map the location and streets you are looking to buy in, you can configure Rightmove to send you emails as soon as properties appear in that area. Many homeowners may continue to use it after they buy a property because it helps them know how the prices are trending in their area.

2- Zoopla.co.uk:

You must also visit this website/app as part of your search. In addition to many of the features that Rightmove offers, you will find some estate agents will choose Zoopla as the means of advertising their properties online. There is clear competition between those two big websites/apps.

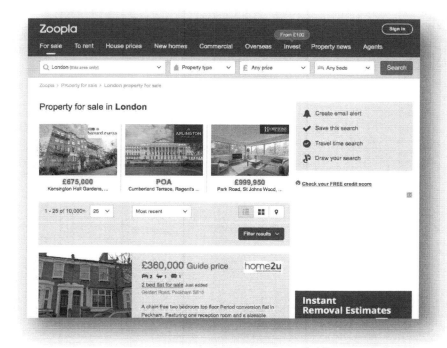

One key feature you will find in Zoopla that as of yet Rightmove does not have is the estimated value of the property. Should you find a property of interest, you can check Zoopla's assessment of the area regarding how much value it has gone up by in last few years. It will also estimate what the value of the property should be now. You can even modify the estimate by stating some of the special features or improvements that the property has had. Usually, their estimates are quite good but they are just estimates.

3- Estate agents:

You will find many estate agents will list a property on their own websites before they list it on Rightmove or Zoopla. This is because there is a cost associated with posting properties on other company's websites/apps as opposed to their own which is virtually free. Therefore check the local area where you intend to buy and ask the estate agents for their website addresses. Check them regularly and see if you can spot anything.

Fact 17:

Some of the best property deals never reach websites because the properties get sold within days of reaching the estate agent.

4- Other websites/apps:

Of course, there are other websites that might list properties of interest to you, but they are not necessarily solely intended for sales of properties and are probably not known for doing so. For instance, ebay.co.uk, gumtree.com and craiglist.com are typical examples. Ebay™ is mostly an auction website, and you are unlikely to find houses on auction. However, more and more estate agents advertise their properties on them probably because it is cheaper. The same goes for Gumtree™ which is a very popular website for searching for jobs and renting properties but is not so popular for selling/buying properties. Finally, Craiglist™ is popular for jobs and personals, but occasionally you find people advertising the sale of properties. Always be careful and make sure you have a lawyer check any purchase. If you are going to buy with a mortgage, then your bank will not allow a purchase to go ahead unless they are sure it is correct and legal.

4.2: Estate Agents:

Registering with an estate agent in areas where you want to buy is a wise step. Now that you know the areas in which you want to buy, you have done your research into the likely prices, and you have a good idea of what you are looking for, you are in a good position to tell the estate agent what you want. Your position will be strengthened if you register with a few estate agents and let each one know that you are doing so. Estate agents want to make sure they sell you something they have. Estate agents usually get a commission of 1% on properties they sell from the seller rather than you. So for selling property of value £150,000, they make at least £1,500. They will, therefore, be desperate to sell properties quickly. What is more, properties that are bargains tend to be sold quickly and may not even reach the estate agent's website or the property selling websites/apps. Building a relationship with the estate agent by being nice to them, friendly, keen, and respectable helps a lot. Legally you cannot and should not try to offer them a bribe. Some investors build really strong contacts with estate agents so that they would be contacted as soon as something amazing comes along. There is nothing wrong with that, as the estate agents' role is to try to sell properties quickly and to whoever wants them. It is difficult to build this contact quickly with your estate agent, but if you know someone who is an estate agent or who works in an estate agent's office, then you could be giving yourself that little bit of an advantage when looking for a bargain. There are however other ways of getting a bargain or getting the best price that we talk about in the next section.

Estate agents offer other services that you should take advantage of. For instance, the estate agent may be able to arrange your mortgage and lawyer. If they can do this, you should take up the offer. Having the estate agent arrange the mortgage and lawyer for your first ever mortgage would increase your chances of getting your mortgage and close the deal faster. Estate agents only get their commission if they sell and hence they will be pushing both bank and lawyer to speed up the work for the sale to be completed.

4.3: Investigating the area before you make an offer

Before you make an offer, you may want to investigate the area to make sure there are no issues. Knock on the doors of a few neighbours and say hello. Tell them you are thinking of buying nearby and ask if they can tell you a bit about the area. You will find that most people are very friendly and will be more than happy to chat. People tend to be honest, and you will get a good feel for the place after speaking to at least three houses. Ask about any disturbances, the crime rate, good schools, new developments, shops, and anything else that concerns you. You will be able to find out some of this information online as well. You can enter the postcode of the address on a variety of websites that can tell you a bit about the area. The websites you can check include propertydetective.com and neighbourhood.statistics.gov.uk. Also, if listed on Zoopla or Rightmove, you will find some statistics next to the property. You can find many more sites online.

4.4: Things that should put you off buying

First of all, check that you can get a 'house insurance' on the property. This can be done online or over the phone. If an area is listed as risky, they will refuse to insure it for you then this is not a good sign. This may mean that the area has a very high crime rate, flood risk, or subsidence problems. The second thing that should put you off is finding many properties with blocked out windows, damaged cars and a lack of families. If this is the only place you can afford, then you could take a gamble, but you will have difficulty selling the property in the future. Inside the property, look out for mould as this may be a sign of a broken pipe or humidity problems that could be quite expensive to fix. A buyer should be aware that uneven doors or walls might also be a sign of subsidence. Finally cracked or falling ceilings maybe signs of roof problems. In any of these cases, you should consider paying a surveyor to make sure there are no serious problems with the property. Mortgage companies will insist you do a survey anyway, so this is good news.

Fact 18:

You will be surprised how much cheaper you can buy a house if it needs a little bit of decoration that would cost a fraction of the saving you can make.

4.5: Things that should not put you off buying

Things like old décor, a messy house, terrible carpets, and dirty walls, broken doors, holes and minor cracks in the wall should be considered cosmetic. Painting, floorings, carpets, new doors and filling cracks are not expensive, but you will find yourself in a strong position to negotiate the price downwards if such works are required. These cosmetic problems put off quite a lot of people and are a sign that the seller, who cannot afford to fix them, is in need of money quickly.

4.6: Buying directly from a Builder

Buying a house that was built a while ago has the advantage that it has stood the test of time. Buying a house that has been built recently, especially if bought from a builder must come with some necessary guarantees. The NHBC warranty and cover is the standard for many builders. This is issued by the National House Building Council in Britain to protect homeowners when purchasing a newly built house. Details of their warranty can be found at www.nhbc.co.uk/Warrantiesandcover/. Only certified builders can get cover, and it protects you if there are serious building issues. Many mortgage companies will not give you a mortgage for a newly built house unless it has the NHBC warranty.

4.7: Getting the bottom price

The price you see listed is not fixed and is not usually the minimum price. The person selling has a lot to decide about the price they wish to sell the property for. They can insist on the price listed, or they can let it go for less, may be 5% to 15% cheaper. There are a few factors at play here, and you should look out for them as they could reduce your mortgage and repayments. Think how much of a saving this could be over a long period of a mortgage. So look out for factors such as:

1. **How long has the property been on the market?** If it has been for more than a month, then you can bet that the seller will accept 5% to 10% less even if the estate agent tells you that they turned down that offer before. A month later, they may take it. You have to play the 'poker' face and pretend you like it but only if the price is right. Otherwise, you will keep looking.

2. **What is the reason for sale?** If they are moving and have found a place already, then they may be desperate for a quick sale. If it is a divorce or death (inheritance), there is even more reason why they would want to sell this quickly. Some of the best bargains were had when people needed to move abroad, divorce quickly or death occurred. Of course, there are also houses that are repossessed by the bank which has the bonus that the bank only cares about getting their money back, so you can make offers and see if they will take them.

3. **Does it require decoration or is the decor outdated?** You would be really surprised how many properties are sold 10% to 30% cheaper because the decor is outdated. Old carpets, old paint, maybe an old kitchen and toilet, all of which may cost £5,000 to £10,000 to put right and yet you could get the property for £30,000 cheaper. What is more, if you are happy to put up with the old decor and slowly replace it yourself or book your own tradesmen, then you

will get the house decorated even cheaper. A bit of patience and dealing with a little hassle can save you a fortune.

4. **Come as a family:** If and when you visit the property and if the owner is on the property, the impression you give makes a huge difference. People do get attached to their properties beyond the fact that they are just bricks. Houses hold for many British people memories and special places in their hearts. They feel that they owe it to the house that it goes to

---

Fact 19:

Very few homeowners expect to sell their property at the asking price. The majority will be ready to accept a 5%-10% reduction even in highly desirable areas.

'someone nice' and why not? Knowing that it is going to a family who will continue to care for the house could seal the deal. If you see that they have a pet, tell them you intend to get a pet. If they have a cat, say you will be getting a cat!

One thing you cannot do is to try to negotiate the price with the owner or ask them to drop the price. You must deal directly with the agent. Also, you should not, under any circumstances, approach the owner on your own. People in the past have tried to bypass the estate agent, and this very rarely works because sellers are extremely nervous about dishonest selling practices and worry about getting into legal trouble with their agents. Do follow the protocols (rules) of buying and selling in the UK. You do not have much to lose as the only person who pays a fee for the sale is the seller, not you. If you are renting, and the landlord wishes to sell the property, and in this case, you can get a small discount (1%) which would be the saving the seller would have had to pay the estate agent. On a property of £200,000, the seller would be saving £2000, and you could both split the saving between you. So the landlord should sell it to you for £199,000.

4.8: Bidding offers:

An American style of selling that seems to have coughed up in recent times in some areas of the UK where the demand is by far surpassed the supply. Namely some city centre areas such as in London. The process works by having many people showing interest in a property, so much so that the estate agent sets one day for all of them to come and view it at the same time. The buyers come all at the same time and look at the property; they then have a deadline that is usually next day midday to put in the offer. The seller usually accepts the highest offer. In theory, it seems to be fair and straightforward. However, we have serious reservations about this way of selling. The pressures are put massively on the buyers to make offers over and above the actual asking price. In fact, as reported in the media, in many cases the prices exceed the asking prices (Clements, 2014). This is because the buyers are put in an intimidating position to compete with other buyers. The process is not transparent enough as it could be open to abuse. Mainly our concern is that the seller might use tactic of inviting friends and family to pretend to want to buy and even pretend they are 'extremely' interested in buying the place so you and other buyers get nervous and make excessive offers. Also you never know if you paid too much for it. You may put an offer that is significantly higher than the next person. All in all, this is probably the best way to sell but not the best way to buy. We think as a first time buyer, you should stay away from any sales like this unless you do not mind just going there and giving a silly offer but not have your hopes pinned too much on getting it.

Chapter 5: Buying the property

In this chapter we look at the final stages of purchasing your property; what is involved in this process, how this process should work and why sometimes it may fail. We will also be advising you what to do if you feel cheated during part of the process.

F inding the right property and getting everything running is just half the job. The second half is to complete the purchase. Before you make an offer to buy a property, you should make sure a bank is willing to give you a loan and that they say yes in response to your first application. We suggest a very good way of achieving this. First get a letter from the bank saying they are willing to lend you 'up to' a certain amount, and then you make your offer. Provided you get the owner to agree on the price, and then you get a lawyer involved. Lawyers have a very important role. In this chapter, we will explain the role of lawyers and some important terms.

5.1: Getting the Mortgage

We emphasized before how important it is not to get a mortgage application declined at the first attempt. There is a way to do that. First of all, make sure you read the earlier chapters on how to get a mortgage and which also identifies the paperwork you need to have ready for the bank. Instead of asking for a certain amount to which they may say 'no', a safer way to approach a bank is to ask if they can offer you any kind of mortgage and, if so, how much. Instead of asking the bank for a mortgage of £100,000 and getting declined, you can ask the bank how much they can lend you and if they say £92,000 then you know this is your limit. In fact, if you follow all the right procedures in applying, the bank will provide you with a letter as to how much they will be willing to lend you. By obtaining this letter you have in your hand a document that confirms, in principle, that the bank will be happy to lend you money. This letter will leave you in a much stronger position when you go looking for properties because the estate agent will know that you are serious and will, therefore, be desperate to persuade you to buy through them. You may even be able to barter for a lower price on a property by explaining that this is the maximum the bank is willing to lend you.

5.2: Getting a Lawyer

We explained before that you could get a lawyer through the estate agency. This does not mean that the lawyer works for the agency. The lawyer should be independent and work for you.

However, estate agents tend to recommend lawyers with whom they have worked before and who they know will work quickly and complete on time. Your lawyer needs to conduct some searches which include requests to the council to make sure that no plans are being made that would affect the property, such as digging, railway, sewage, or road construction. These can seriously affect the value of the property. Searches are not expensive and so should be carried out. In addition to these searches, your lawyer will communicate directly with your mortgage lender, will take your deposit and hold on to it until the selling date. The lawyer will also communicate with the seller's lawyer to agree on a completion date. Lawyers will even hold the fees for the agency. Lawyers have a lot of work to do and will therefore typically charge a fixed fee for buying or selling of a house. Typically a lawyer would charge anything between £600 and £2000. You should try to negotiate a fixed price from the start. Some mortgage companies in the past have offered to pay the legal fees or add the lawyer's fees to the mortgage to help first-time buyers. Some banks may still do it, so check with your bank - it does not hurt to ask.

5.3: Making an Offer

Please note that depending on where you are in the UK can make a difference here. In Scotland, making an offer to buy a place is considered legally binding. Usually, your lawyer would contact the lawyer of the seller, and by exchange of letters (called missives), you become legally responsible for buying it. If the purchase does not go ahead, the seller can legally sue you for any losses. In England, Wales and Northern Ireland, the contract is not completed until the 'exchange of contracts' takes place, which is usually near the end of the process.

If for any reason the buyer cannot go ahead with the purchase or changes their mind, the seller cannot sue them for any losses. This may not seem significant but in the process of buying it can make a difference. In Scotland, you have to be very careful before you make an offer that you may regret.

Wherever you are in the UK, you can try your luck with few low offers. You can, in theory, make as many offers as you like but be careful not to upset the owner and estate agent by giving them the impression that you are just playing a game. Think of the issues that we listed in the previous chapter. We would always recommend you start with an offer that is at least 10% lower than the asking price. For instance, if the sellers are asking for £110,000, then logic dictates that they will likely accept an offer of £99,000. If you feel that they are in a hurry, have been waiting for a very long time, or if any of the other issues we highlighted in Chapter 4 apply, then offer £95,000, then perhaps £98,000 and wait and see what happens. Again there are some exceptions, mostly you will see in Scotland, as most of the times properties are listed with a title indicating what the seller is willing to consider:

> "Offers Over" which means the seller will not be likely to consider anything less than the price listed and is hoping for a higher price.
> "Fixed Price" which means the seller will not consider any other price.
> "Offers in the region" which means the seller could consider prices below the listed price.

If the property is new and has just been listed, the seller will not be likely to accept a drop of 10%, especially if you are the first person to make an offer. This then falls on you, how much you feel this property matters to you and if you feel the difference of 10% is not worth the risk of losing the property to someone else. If this were the case, then we would recommend you make an offer for the full price or near the full price.

Ultimately, only the seller can decide if they will accept the offer. If they accept it, then you have a deal. The deal, however, will not be completed until some further paperwork and checks are completed.

Fact 20:

The home report is reviewed by the mortgage company, your lawyer and yourself. If there is anything serious you will be informed.

5.4: Property Survey

Once the offer is made and accepted, you will instruct your lawyer and the mortgage company that you have now a property of interest. The mortgage company will set a date for the property to be surveyed independently by a surveyor. Usually, you will be given a choice between a basic and a detailed survey and the difference in price is significant. The basic survey can cost from £150 to £250 whereas a detailed survey might cost as much as £1000. The mortgage companies are usually happy with a basic survey unless the basic survey comes back with some major concerns about the property. Major concerns usually mean that they suspect structural problems with the property, such as possible subsidence or a building in a poor state of repair. Having a survey carried out is very important because if there are any structural problems, these can be very expensive to fix.

Be assured though that these kinds of problem are very rare in the UK. The standards of building, maintenance and insurance cover means that if a property ever has suffered any serious problems, then they are likely to have been fixed by the time the property reaches the market. The only exception to this would be an auctioned property in which case you should ask a builder/surveyor to inspect the property before you try to buy it. They will tell you how long and how much it would cost to fix if there are any serious problems.

There is no need to worry as in the absolute majority of cases the basic survey comes back as 'very good', and the bank is happy to lend money on the property. This means that you can move to the next stage.

5.5: Exchange and Completion dates

You will hear these terms when the property purchase is moving towards to a closing date. The term 'exchange date' refers to the day your lawyer and the seller's lawyer agrees to exchange contracts and that the purchase is to be completed, i.e. the property title is transferred from the seller to you and you finally get the keys from the estate agent. Sometimes the buyer or the seller needs some extra time between the exchange and completion because they have to make some arrangements to deal with furniture, rent arrangements, or perhaps because they cannot yet move into the property they are buying because the exchange date is set to a different date than the completion date. Sometimes both the buyer and seller are in a hurry and want everything completed quickly, so they are both happy to set the exchange and completion date on the same day. This is what we would usually recommend.

5.6: Getting the keys

Getting the keys can be an exciting moment but the first day in your new property has to be about making sure that the seller has moved all their stuff and left the property in a clean and tidy state. If any damage has occurred or major rubbish has been left behind you should contact your lawyer immediately who will report it to the buyer's lawyer. It is also normal for the seller to disconnect the electricity, water and phone services. You can, however, ring any company, including the company that previously provided services to the property and ask them to reconnect you. Within hours you should have these services running again.

5.7: Your first mortgage payments and future payments

You can always agree with your mortgage company the day of the month on which you wish to make your mortgage payments. Never set it at the end of the month as this may be at a time when you are short of money. Instead, set it a few days after you usually get paid. Mortgage companies are flexible, but this means your first mortgage payment may be a little higher. Let's say you completed on the 25th of the month and you asked the mortgage company to charge you on the 1st of each month. In this case, the mortgage company will not have enough time to set the first payment on the 1st of the month but the following month will charge you a month plus 5 days. The same applies if you complete on the 15th of the month, then the following month you will be charged a month plus 15 days. This is why the first payment is usually a little more money, but you will quickly get into the routine of making the usual payments each month.

5.8: Who to complaint to

If you feel cheated at any stage of the process, be that by the estate agent, the mortgage company, the surveyors or builders you can approach the Property Ombudsman. The Property Ombudsman is an independent government organisation that aims to provide consumer protection to homebuyers and sellers, landlords and tenants. The Property Ombudsman provides platform-independent conflict resolution, seeks to raise standards of service in the residential property industry and publishes codes of conduct governing how organisations deal when exchange, sales and renting of properties. You can read more about the Property Ombudsman or file a complaint at www.tpos.co.uk.

5.9: Housing Market and Brexit:

There is uncertainty in the housing market in the UK at the moment. The vote to leave the EU has come as a surprise even for those who supported it. And for many people planning to buy a property, there have been some concerns and here is why. The UK leaving the EU will have an impact on the UK economy. As of yet, no one is sure how the UK will leave the EU and how this will affect the UK economy. Those who supported the move insist that this will help the UK economy because it will allow the UK to negotiate trade deals with the rest of the world. They also argue that the EU will want to have open trade with the UK because of the UK imports more from the EU than exports to the EU. It is, therefore, argued that the UK will do fine if not better outside the EU. They point to examples of Norway and Switzerland as two countries that are outside the EU but trade and have access to EU markets. On the other hands, those who support staying part of the EU insist that the financial sector, a very strong contributor to the UK economy along with investments and trades, will impact the UK economy negatively if the UK leaves the EU. Most economists agree this is the case. Restricting EU nationals' movements will also impact the economy and business, including the housing market. Just imagine one million EU citizen asked to leave how this would impact everything from trading, shopping, farming, manufacturing, renting, and house prices.

On the whole, we agree with many experts that indicate that housing market is slowing down but will maintain a slow growth. This means that house prices are expected to continue to go up but slowly. Since the vote, there has not been a rush of selling or panic as some may have expected. In fact, 2016 saw an overall increase in house prices even after the Brexit vote. What has contributed to this? The drop in the British Pound exchange rate has made British exports, inwards tourism, and services around 20% cheaper for foreigners. Foreign investors in everything from the stock market to house property are finding with the exchange rate these investments are around 20% cheaper too. But these are expected to be short-term and will soften the blow that would have otherwise shaken the British economy and housing market significantly. Here are some key indicators we are looking for and believe will determine how the UK housing market will move in the coming months and years.

5.9.1. Demand for housing:

Many people blamed the credit crunch for the housing market drop in the US and the UK back in 2008. And while this is true, the roots of the housing market drop is that many businesses could not borrow money so some failed or while others had to down size, resulting in an increase in unemployment rates. Unemployment meant many people were not able to pay their mortgages and banks were no longer lending people money. And all this cascaded into a drop in demand on housing, leading to a price crash in the US and a drop in house prices in the UK. This represents an example of how demand drops. But this does not happen overnight, and it takes time. Some people fear Brexit is heading the UK economy in that same direction. If the UK businesses are not allowed to trade freely with Europe, then they will either close down or downsize, result in higher unemployment rates, and this will cascade to lower demand on houses; ending up with a drop in house prices.

EU citizens living in the UK: There are no indications that EU citizens working in the UK will be asked to leave. Immigration figures show that there is already a drop in the number of EU citizens living or moving to the UK (Office of National Statistics, 2017). Even if we take the extreme assumption that overnight the UK government decides to treat all EU citizens as 'foreigners'; you will find that under the UK immigration rules, the majority of EU citizen who has jobs will qualify immediately to get work permits. Many EU citizens have been more than four years in the UK; this means they would qualify for 'Indefinite Leave to Remain' or even 'British Citizenship'. However, this has to be a key indicator to look out for. Minor drops or increases will not have any major impact, but anything more significant would most definitely impact demand for housing. Since buying property in the UK is open to anyone, even foreigners, then naturally demand from EU citizens living in the UK to buy or rent will continue far into the future. Also, keep in mind that the protection that is offered from unemployment benefits including housing support if you become unemployed applies to anyone who pays taxes into the system. Therefore, EU citizens living and working in the UK will continue to benefit from the same protections they had before.

5.9.2. The economy after Brexit:

Financial sector access to the EU market is the prize money the UK has achieved being part of the EU. London has become the world centre of financial transactions, banking, and insurance brokerage due to its open access to the EU market. While this may seem not so important for the average person on the street, it is significant. This access has contributed significantly to the UK economy and the boom in the housing market in London and beyond. Taxes collected directly and indirectly from these financial transactions and the people they employ, contribute a large amount of money that has been used in everything from welfare, defence, and education budgets. If the UK leaves the single market and more so loses its access to the EU financial markets, then we should expect many banks, financial institutions, and company headquarters either relocating or downsizing their operations in the UK. The knock on effect will be significant. Relocating and downsizing will mean job losses, less tax collected, and less funding. It will have the same effects as the credit crash of 2008. This is not a doom scenario as some may fear. One of several options will likely to happen. Either the British government will find a new EU deal or international deals that will help balance the economy. Otherwise, the British people will vote in political parties who will take the UK back into the EU- namely look out for any significant surge in Liberal Democrat votes in the next general election. As humiliating as this may seem to the national pride if the economy is doing bad and people fear they would lose their homes then they will have to do what it takes to get the economy moving again.

5.9.3. Interest rates going up:

With interest rates at 0.5% (half of 1 percent), there is really little room left for interest rates to go any lower than this. In fact, in 2017, we saw the first rise in interest rates in more than 10 years. The only fear that some people have is that interest rates may continue to go up. Inflation is likely to force Bank of England to start increasing interest rates. This will slow the housing market prices. Bank of England will do what it can to minimise the negative impact on the housing market. How people feel about their homes in the UK affects every aspect of the UK economy. If you are worried, then you have several options at your disposal including finding a long-term fixed interest rate mortgage. Some homeowners are able to find mortgage interest rates that are fixed for 2, 3, 4, or even 5 years. Then sit back and see how the Brexit vote plays out. In fact, it is now the authors' preferred advice is to select a long-term fixed rate that you can afford and is less than what you used to pay in rent.

Having cold feet feeling about this? You should not. The rules of buying have not changed. If you are going to pay less monthly for buying than renting, then you really cannot go wrong. Go back to chapter 1 and remember that you cannot lose your house provided you do everything properly and legally. If house prices go down, this should not affect you. You will continue to live in the house that you own and incrementally own more of it every month.

5.10: Final Thoughts

The concept of buying a property in the UK is a long and old tradition. The UK market is probably the most mature market in this area. From that people in the UK use the term 'Property ladder' which you and almost every first-time buyer are likely to do.

Property ladder means your first house is not likely to be big enough, near enough, or nice enough to be the one you will live for a very long time. In fact, it is almost always the case that you will find that your first property will have to be selected with lots of compromises. It is likely to be a one bedroom flat in an area not terribly nice and far from good public transport. And this should not put you off. This is what happens again and again. The sooner you start on that ladder, the sooner you can start moving up the ladder.

In two to five years time, you would have proved yourself to mortgage companies and thus you are able to get better rates. In that period as well you would have built some equity into the property on top of the deposit you have put. You will also find your income from job promotions has increased. With bigger deposit, better credit history, and improved income, you can move up to a one-bedroom house or two-bedroom flat in a nicer area. If your finances jump up significantly, then you can consider just renting out the first property and moving to a nicer place while the rent of the first property helps to top up your income.

However, of course, this could go wrong way if you mess up your credit history, borrow too much against your property, and do little or no improvements to the property. Taking irresponsible actions like these will mean you may end up never moving up or worse so losing the property and go back to renting.

Much of this is in your own hands. Make this investment work for you and if anything goes wrong then go back to chapter one and read how you can protect yourself. We are always keen to hear about your experiences and what we can do to improve the book. Visit our official website at www.MyUKHouse.co.uk.

References:

Chalabi, M. (2013) 'Mortgages: how many Britons have one, and how much do they owe?', *The Guardian*. Available at: http://www.citethemrightonline.com/digital-internet/the-internet/blogs (Accessed: 13 March 2014)

Clements, L. (2014) *What is really like to be first-time buyer in London.* Available at: https://uk.finance.yahoo.com/news/what-it-s-really-like-to-be-a-first-time-buyer-in-london-144921870.html (Accessed: 8 June 2014)

CML (2013) *'Arrears and repossessions continue to fall, says CML'.* Available at: http://www.cml.org.uk/cml/media/press/3731 (Accessed: 13 March 2014)

Daily Mail (2013) *London Property Prices 1973-2012.* Available at: http://i.dailymail.co.uk/i/pix/2012/04/04/article-0-12766978000005DC-74_634x389.jpg (Accessed: 13 March 2014)

Experian (2014) *Screenshot of website.* Available at: http://www.experian.co.uk/assets/consumer/credit-score/images/score-screen/CE-your-score.png (Accessed: 8 June 2014)`

GOV.UK (2014) *Rent a room scheme.* Available at: http://www.hmrc.gov.uk/individuals/tmarent-a-room-scheme.shtml (Accessed: 23 May 2014)

Gunn, E. (2013) *Can a bad credit history REALLY put you on the lending blacklist? Credit rating facts and fictions.* Available at: http://www.thisismoney.co.uk/money/cardsloans/article-2514374/Credit-rating-myths-Can-bad-history-REALLY-blacklist.html (Accessed: 1 June 2014)

HMRC (2017) *Stamp Duty Land Tax rate and thresholds.* Available at: http://www.hmrc.gov.uk/tools/sdlt/land-and-property.htm (Accessed: 14 January 2018)

Mortgage Advise Bureau (2014) *Choose the right mortgage.* Available at: http://www.mortgageadvicebureau.com/choose-the-right-mortgage/ (Accessed: 05 April 2014)

Office of National Statistics (2017) *Migration Statistics Quarterly Report: November 2017.* Available at: https://www.ons.gov.uk/peoplepopulationandcommunity/populationandmigration/internationalmigration/bulletins/migrationstatisticsquarterlyreport/november2017 (Accessed: 12/01/2018)

Uren A. (2013) *I moved to Italy years ago and forgot about my credit card debts. But how they tracked me down. Do I have to pay up?* Available at: http://www.thisismoney.co.uk/money/experts/article-2373457/Do-I-pay-old-credit-card-debts.html (Accessed: 6 April 2014)

The diagram below visually splits essential steps to get mortgage. Every step is numbered.

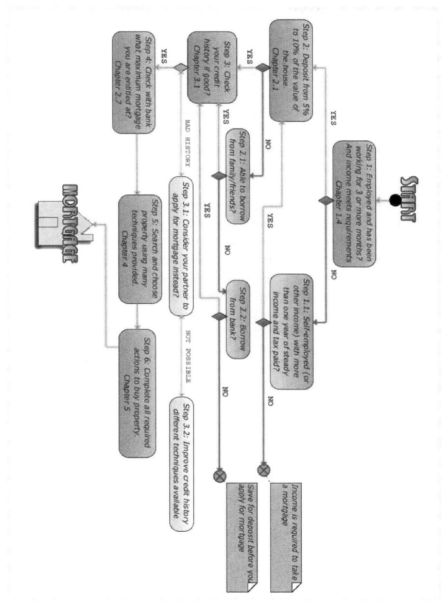

37783358R00066

Printed in Great Britain
by Amazon